New Recipes for the

Cuisinart® food processor

by James Beard and Carl Jerome

Director James Beard Cooking Classes

D1042976

Copyright© 1976 and 1978 by Cuisinarts Inc.
ISBN 0-936662-00-X

Printed in the United States of America
Cuisinart is a trademark of Cuisinarts Inc.

Contents

Introduction

Several years ago I visited a restaurant owned by a friend of mine, Georges Garin, in the South of France. The restaurant was closed but four of us prepared dinner in the kitchen. We were making a stuffing to force under the skin of two chickens to be roasted and we used a machine that I had never seen before to chop the mushrooms and crumbs and other ingredients that went into the stuffing. I was filled with awe and wonder at this incredible machine which had, in nothing flat, chopped the mushrooms as fine as one wanted. It chopped shallots and made crumbs. It was remarkable!

I was on my way home so I at once found the name of the manufacturer and the shipper. Directly upon my return to New York, I had one ordered and delivered to my home. It was a very proud day when it arrived. I really spent almost twelve hours playing with it and trying it out on all manner of things. There was a small book with it, in French, that suggested a group of ideas for which it could be used. I'm sure I tried every one of them and thought of a number of things the book didn't express.

At any rate, it was one of the most profitable play days I have ever put in and I have been using the machine ever since. It's now known as the Cuisinart Food Processor. It's an unbelievable success across the country, which has cheered me because I realize that there are still some kitchen snobs who will not accept the fact that modern technological perfections are to be used and not talked about. I'm perfectly certain were Escoffier or Montagné alive today, they would be happy to use a food processor. I have no patience with people who say: "It doesn't quite do what you can do by hand". Well, I say: "The hell with it!". If it isn't quite as perfectly chopped or as evenly chopped as by hand, is it really going to make that much difference in the finished dish, and is it a crime to cut down your timing on a recipe because you have something that is faster than the human hand? It's all very well to chop by hand, it's all very well to pulverize in a mortar and pestle, but if you can find a machine that will do it for you, why not? A great many people have agreed "Why not?", and are using it with greater and greater breadth of imagination. The Cuisinarts people believe in it as strongly as anyone could and their constant pursuit of new ways to use it and of making it more beneficial to their clients is most refreshing. Their assistance to

3

Carl Jerome and to me in preparing this book has been endless. They will try a recipe nineteen times if there are little variations that they think might improve it.

Let's evaluate this piece of equipment and see what it really does for you. It will chop practically anything; it will chop meat and, if you are intelligent about using your machine and turning it rapidly on and off and on and off, you can gauge pretty well the size of chop you want. If you're chopping meat for hamburgers, let us say, you can have coarsely chopped or finely chopped or medium chopped, as you wish, by watching and controlling the processing. It will chop vegetables. It will chop nuts. Its chopping proclivities are tremendous and almost endless. With the shredding and slicing attachments, there's very little you can't imagine as labor-saving and time-saving procedures—for example, shredding potatoes, cabbage and cheese and slicing carrots, onions and cucumbers.

The food processor will not liquefy, but it will pulverize certain things. It will make a peanut butter or an almond butter of any particular texture by merely going on or stopping or by adding things as you will notice in the recipes to come. It will blend things together. You can make a beautiful herb butter or a spiced butter. Or, you can make a hard sauce with various ingredients in it.

It's a perfect tool for sauces. It makes incredibly good emulsified sauces—mayonnaise, rémoulade, aioli: all of these which are so dependent upon proper emulsification to make them perfect, are stars in the food processor. It will blend other sauces extremely well and it will combine sauces. You can combine to make a mustard mayonnaise or you can combine to make a cocktail sauce. It is, in addition to being a maker, a combiner.

It will combine ingredients, such as for steak tartare, all at one time. The meat, the seasonings, the whole thing, and you have a completely constructed steak tartare in nothing flat. Here again, one must turn the processor on and off while watching to control the size of the chop. This is very important.

One of the greatest things the food processor does is to make pastry. Having taught for over twenty-five years, I know how badly many people make pastry and how often they feel they cannot improve. This is almost completely foolproof and makes beautiful, beautiful pastry. In a matter of twenty-six seconds you have a pâte brisée for your tarts. In forty seconds you have a very rich tart pastry. It's infallible as far as pastry is concerned, if you are infallible. It goes further, it makes bread. It makes brioche. It is limited in that it will not make a big batch of bread, but it will make one perfectly good loaf. It will make a small quantity of brioche.

Yes, there are things this machine will not do. It will not grind coffee. It will not beat egg whites. Or, rather it will beat egg whites, but not with volume because the blade is not an aerator—egg whites need aeration to be perfect. It will make a heavy whipped cream but not a fluffy, light schlag if that is what you're looking for. It will not give you perfect blending of herbs and various other mixtures, if you want them almost liquefied. It does not make satisfactory butter. It's limited in its capacity and you must be careful not to overload it.

The recipes we have given on the ensuing pages are styled for the machine. Don't add more, the machine does most things so fast that it's easy to make several batches. Once you have looked at the machine and its construction, once you have worked with it, you will soon understand what quantities to use for any recipe.

An interesting part of this little book is the number of grand meals that one can execute from the recipes featured. You can take a whole dinner party, or a Christmas dinner or a Thanksgiving dinner, and plan it around your food processor. You will cut down your labor in a tremendous fashion, to the point where you will almost halve your preparation time for the full meal.

In the book, we are fortunate to have contributions from a number of people who are familiar to everyone in the food business. I'm happy to thank this group: Craig Claiborne, Helen McCully, Jacques Pépin, Simone Beck, Julie Dannenbaum and all the other great names in the food world that you will encounter on these pages for their kindness and generosity in giving us recipes. The recipes are unusual and smack of these personalities, which is an important factor.

Use your Cuisinart Food Processor to the hilt. You are going to find a few pages of very serious directions as to how to best manage your unit. After you have become used to it and have prepared a great variety of dishes, start experimenting on your own. This is one of the exciting parts of working with the food processor—to start using it in new ways for new things. Have great joy in cooking and preparing your dishes with the processor.

James A. Beard

Guest Contributors

Simone Beck is the wonderful French woman who co-authored with Julia Child *Mastering the Art of French Cooking, Volumes I and II.* Her most recent book is *Simca's Cuisine.* Madame Beck conducts cooking classes from her home in France. She has also taught classes in New York and the San Francisco Bay area.

Craig Claiborne is one of America's leading food authorities. Mr. Claiborne is the food editor of the New York Times and the author of six cookbooks, the most recent of which is *Craig Claiborne's Favorites from The New York Times.* His recipes are always varied, interesting and exciting.

John Clancy is the executive test chef for the Time-Life series, *Foods of the World.* Previously, Mr. Clancy was chef at the Coach House, one of America's finest restaurants, located in Greenwich Village. He is the author of *John Clancy's Baking Book* which includes baking recipes that he teaches in his baking classes.

Julie Dannenbaum is the founding director of the Creative Cooking School located in Philadelphia, Pennsylvania. This is one of America's largest and most successful cooking schools. Mrs. Dannenbaum is the author of *Julie Dannenbaum's Creative Cooking School Cookbook* and *Menus for All Occasions.*

Pierre Franey was born in Burgundy and apprenticed to a restaurant in France at age 16. He was Henri Soulé's first associate at New York's legendary restaurant, Le Pavillon. He became executive chef in 1950. Since the disappearance of Le Pavillon, he has become an officer of a major food company and he is a frequent contributor to the food pages of the New York Times and other publications.

Marcella Hazan is America's foremost teacher of Italian cooking. Her cooking school, located in New York, stresses Northern Italian cooking. Mrs. Hazan is the author of the *Classic Italian Cookbook* and her recipes have appeared in numerous newspapers and magazines throughout the United States.

Madhur Jaffrey is the stunning Indian actress who has won the Berlin Film Festival award as Best Actress. Mrs. Jaffrey established herself as a cooking expert when she wrote the book, *An Invitation to Indian Cookery,* which was published in 1973 by Knopf. Mrs. Jaffrey teaches courses in Indian cookery at the James Beard Cooking Classes.

Barbara Kafka's articles on food and wine have appeared in magazines and newspapers throughout the country. Mrs. Kafka edited and wrote the recipes and notes for *The Art of Cuisine,* containing the recipes and graphics of Toulouse Lautrec. She was also editor-in-chief of *The Cooks' Catalog,* one of the most important volumes ever written on kitchen equipment. Mrs. Kafka is a member of the faculty of the James Beard Cooking Classes.

Loni Kuhn is a noted West Coast cooking school teacher and author of *A Cook's Tour,* a monthly newsletter of international recipes and cooking tips.

Leon Lianides is the owner-proprieter of the Coach House, one of America's finest restaurants, located in Greenwich Village in New York.

Helen McCully is recognized as one of the most influential food people in America today. She is food editor of House Beautiful magazine and author of many cookbooks including *Nobody Ever Tells You These Things About Food and Drink,* based on her magazine column "Nobody Ever Tells You These Things", and *Waste Not, Want Not,* a cookbook of delicious food from leftovers. Miss McCully has appeared in demonstrations and lectures across the country and was formerly food editor of McCall's magazine. She is a member of the faculty of the Good Cooking School.

Perla Meyers is the author of two recent cookbooks, *Seasonal Cookery* and *From the Peasant Kitchen.* She also conducts cooking classes from her New York home.

Jacques Pépin is the monthly columnist for House Beautiful magazine. Formerly chef to General DeGaulle, Mr. Pepin is author of *Chez Moi, a French Cook Cooks at Home.* Mr. Pepin has given demonstrations around the country and teaches regularly in the New York area.

Maurice Moore-Betty is the founding director of The Moore-Betty School of Cooking in New York. He is the author of two cookbooks, *Cooking for Occasions* and *The Moore-Betty Cooking School of Fine Cooking,* and, most recently, co-author of *Mary Poppins in the Kitchen.*

Andre Soltner is the owner-proprietor of America's finest French restaurant, New York's Lutèce. He is considered by many to be the finest French chef in the United States and is one of only two people in the United States to hold the coveted award from the French government, the Meilleur Ouvrier de France.

About Your Food

These pages are not a substitute for the instruction manual that came with your Cuisinart food processor. Before you even plug in your machine, read the instructions carefully and thoroughly. In fact, read the operating instructions and the technique section twice. Your machine will give you years of safe, trouble-free service if you operate it according to the instructions. Everyone in your household who has access to the machine should be completely familiar with the instruction manual.

The recipes in this cook book can be prepared in any Cuisinart food processor. They were developed for a standard-size machine without an expanded feed tube.

If you have a larger model, you can process more food at one time than is possible with the standard model. You can therefore often ignore instructions directing you to prepare part of a recipe in batches.

If your machine has an expanded feed tube, you can slice whole fruits and vegetables like oranges, potatoes, onions and peppers. You can therefore generally ignore instructions directing you to halve or quarter such fruits or vegetables to fit the feed tube.

If you have questions about the capability of your machine, refer to your instruction manual. It contains full details about how much food the machine can handle in one batch and the correct techniques for chopping, slicing and shredding.

The following reminders refer to all Cuisinart models.

The Work Bowl
Throughout this book, the work bowl is called the "beaker", an alternate term for it.

The Metal Blade
This is the master tool, the one you use for chopping, puréeing and mixing. It chops raw or cooked food as coarse or fine as you wish. It is almost unbelievably fast in operation. Unless you want a perfectly smooth consistency, stop to check every few seconds, the first time you make a recipe. Otherwise, you are likely to end up with a purée or a powder.

As a general rule, cut ingredients into pieces of 1-inch or smaller before adding them to the work bowl. Turn the machine on and immediately off. Repeat when all the food has fallen to the bottom of the work bowl. Do this a few times. This produces a more even chop. You can then let the machine run until the food reaches the consistency you want.

The Dough Blade
This blade, especially designed for mixing and kneading bread dough, rotates in a way that produces thoroughly and uniformly kneaded dough. Because it does not

Processor

extend to the edge of the work bowl, it does not pick up all the flour when processing small amounts of dough. Use it only when doubling recipes in this book, or for recipes that call for more than 3½ cups of flour.

The Slicing Disc
This disc will convert fruits and vegetables as hard as beets and as soft as strawberries into thin, uniform slices. It will also slice sausages, cooked meat, well chilled raw meat and even butter, if the stick is very cold.

The Shredding Disc
This disc will shred well chilled Cheddar, Swiss and other semi-soft and semi-hard cheese into long, fine shreds. It will do the same for carrots, parsnips, zucchini and many other vegetables.

Handle parts carefully
The metal blade and the discs are very sharp. Handle them carefully and store them, like sharp knives, out of reach of children.

Always make sure that the blade or disc is as far down on the motor shaft as it can go. Rotate it around the shaft until it drops into place.

Be careful not to cut yourself
Always use the pusher when slicing or shredding. Never put your fingers in the feed tube. Always wait until the blade or disc has stopped spinning before removing the cover.

Do not overfill the work bowl
Your instruction book tells you the bowl capacity for thin and thick liquids. The thicker the liquid, the more of it the machine can handle. If you are working close to the machine capacity, be sure to remove the work bowl from the base as soon as you finish processing. This causes the blade to drop down and form an almost perfect seal against the opening.

Empty work bowl carefully
Always remove the work bowl from the base *before* removing the metal blade. This prevents liquid or other food from spilling onto the top of the base.

Avoid tipping the work bowl so far that the blade can fall out. Since it is not attached to the motor shaft, the blade can slip off when the bowl is held at a sharp angle.

Maintenance
Keep the base clean by wiping it with a damp cloth, or use a cleaner like Fantastik or Formula 409. The bowl and cover are made of shatter-resistant, heat-resistant Lexan plastic, and they are dishwasher safe, as are the blades, discs and pushers. Be sure to place the parts in the dishwasher so they cannot fall to the floor and contact the heating element.

Hors d'oeuvre

Kibbeh

¾ **cup fine bulgur***
2 **pounds lean boneless lamb, cut in 1-inch pieces**
1 **small onion, cut in 4 pieces**
   Salt and freshly ground pepper
½ **teaspoon crushed dried mint** *or*
1 **tablespoon chopped fresh mint**
   Parsley sprigs
   Green onions

Wash bulgur and let it soak in cold water for 10 minutes. Pour into strainer lined with cheesecloth and drain thoroughly. With the metal blade in place, add ¼ of the lamb, the bulgur and the onion to the beaker of the food processor. Process, turning on and off, until mixture is evenly combined. Season to taste with salt, pepper and mint. Process until well mixed. Transfer to a large bowl. Repeat 3 times. Combine mixtures by hand. Taste and adjust seasoning.

Transfer mixture to a serving bowl. Cover with plastic wrap and chill several hours. When ready to serve, chop parsley and green onions in processor using the metal blade, and sprinkle over meat mixture. Accompany with small slices of rye or pumpernickel bread. Makes about 4 cups.

* Bulgur is cracked wheat available at Near Eastern and other specialty food stores. If coarse bulgur only is available, process 30 seconds with metal blade, then follow recipe.

Jacques Pépin's Terrine de Foies de Volaille

(Chicken Liver Terrine)

1 medium onion, cut
  in half
1 pound chicken
  livers, trimmed of
  nerves
½ teaspoon salt
1 cup chicken stock
  (about)
1½ cups sweet butter,
  softened and cut
  in pieces
¾ teaspoon Cognac
1¼ teaspoons salt
¾ teaspoon freshly
  ground white
  pepper
½ cup heavy cream
1 envelope unflavored
  gelatin
1 egg white, lightly
  beaten
  Truffle

With the slicing disk in place, cover the beaker and stand onion halves upright in the feed tube. Slice, using moderate pressure on pusher. Combine onion slices, chicken livers and the ½ teaspoon salt in saucepan (do not use aluminum or the stock will discolor) with enough stock to barely cover. Bring to boil. Reduce heat and simmer, covered, for 10 minutes. Remove from heat and let stand for 10 minutes, then strain through a colander, reserving the poaching liquid.

With the metal blade in place, add onion-liver mixture, butter, Cognac, the 1¼ teaspoons salt and the pepper to the beaker. Process until smooth. Transfer to a bowl and refrigerate for 15 minutes. Mix well and refrigerate again for 15 minutes. Mix again. Whip cream until stiff and fold into mixture. Pour into an earthenware terrine or serving dish, seal with plastic wrap and refrigerate.

For aspic, strain reserved poaching liquid (about 1 cup) through cheesecloth or paper towel into saucepan. Stir in gelatin. Add egg white and place over low heat until mixture comes to boil, stirring constantly to prevent scorching. As soon as liquid boils (a layer of scum will form on top), strain through double layer of cheesecloth or sieve lined with paper towels. There should be ¾ cup of very clear liquid. Let cool.

Decorate top of terrine with small pieces of truffle or, if preferred, red tomatoes and the green of a leek, blanched, or any vegetable cutouts that will make the terrine attractive. When aspic is cool and the consistency of heavy syrup, pour a layer on the terrine. Let cool 4 or 5 hours before serving.

Pour any remaining aspic into a non-metal baking dish, chosen so that the aspic will be about ¼-inch thick. Refrigerate, and when firm, cut into small cubes. Use to garnish each serving. Use a spoon to serve terrine and accompany with thin toast. Makes about 6 cups.

Shrimp Balls

15 water chestnuts
1 pound raw, shelled,
  deveined shrimp
1½ tablespoons
  cornstarch
½ teaspoon salt
1 egg
2 tablespoons sherry

With the metal blade in place, add the water chestnuts, shrimp, cornstarch and salt to the beaker. Process, turning on and off rapidly for 15 seconds. Add the egg and sherry and process until a smooth mixture forms. Shape into 1-inch balls. Fry in deep fat at 375 degrees until brown. Drain on paper towels and immediately sprinkle with additional salt. If desired, serve with hot mustard and duck sauce. Makes about 40.

Steak Tartare

1 **pound beef (sirloin or fillet), cut in 1-inch cubes**
6 **anchovy fillets (optional)**
1 **small onion, cut in 8 pieces**
1 **egg yolk**
2 **tablespoons Cognac**
1 **tablespoon capers, drained**
1 **teaspoon salt**
¼ **teaspoon pepper**
2 **or 3 drops Tabasco**

Remove the fat and sinew from meat. With the metal blade in place, add ½ pound beef, 3 anchovy fillets, ½ the onion, egg yolk, 1 tablespoon Cognac, ½ tablespoon capers, ½ teaspoon salt, 1/8 teaspoon pepper and a drop or two of Tabasco to the beaker. Process, turning on and off rapidly, until meat is chopped to desired texture, about 10 to 12 seconds. Do not process until smooth. Steak Tartare should have a somewhat coarse grind. Transfer meat mixture to a bowl. Repeat with remaining ingredients. Combine mixtures and mix well by hand. Makes about 2 cups.

Tiny Cheese Puffs

2 **ounces Swiss or Gruyère cheese, cut in cubes (½ cup)**
⅔ **cup water**
¼ **cup butter, cut in pieces**
1 **tablespoon sugar**
½ **teaspoon salt**
1 **cup all-purpose flour**
4 **large eggs**
1 **egg, beaten
Cucumber or Chicken Fillings (optional; recipes follow)**

With the metal blade in place, add the cheese to the beaker. Process, turning on and off rapidly, until evenly but coarsely chopped. Remove and set aside. Combine water, butter, sugar and salt in saucepan. Bring to boil, stirring occasionally. (Butter should melt before water reaches a boil.) Reduce heat and add flour all at once, stirring vigorously until flour is absorbed and mixture leaves sides of pan and forms a ball, about 1 to 2 minutes. Remove from heat and let cool for about 5 minutes.

Reinsert metal blade. Transfer the batter to the beaker and process for 10 to 15 seconds. Add the 4 eggs all at once and process until smooth and shiny, about 30 to 45 seconds. Add cheese and process, turning on and off, for 5 seconds to combine. Using 2 teaspoons, drop ½-teaspoon portions of batter on ungreased baking sheets, allowing considerable room for expansion during baking. Brush tops with beaten egg and set aside for 5 minutes before baking.

Bake in preheated 425 degree oven for 10 minutes. Reduce heat to 375 degrees and bake for another 10 to 15 minutes or until crisp and golden brown. Let cool completely on wire racks before storing in an airtight container. These also freeze successfully. To crisp before serving, heat in a 350 degree oven for 5 minutes. Serve plain or cut off tops, fill with suggested fillings and replace tops. Makes about 10 dozen.

Cucumber Filling

1 large cucumber,
  peeled, seeded and
  cut in 1-inch pieces
6 parsley sprigs
1 small onion, halved
Salt and pepper to
  taste
Mayonnaise

With the metal blade in place, add cucumber, parsley, onion, salt and pepper to the beaker. Process, turning on and off rapidly, until finely chopped. Be careful not to overprocess. Stir in only enough mayonnaise to bind.

Chicken Filling

¼ cup blanched
  almonds
1 cup cut-up (1-inch
  pieces) cooked
  chicken, skin and
  bones removed
  (about 1½ breasts)
½ cup quartered,
  cooked
  mushrooms
2 tablespoons
  mayonnaise
  (about)
Salt and pepper to
  taste
Dash of nutmeg

With the metal blade in place, add almonds, chicken, mushrooms, mayonnaise, salt, pepper and nutmeg to the beaker. Process, turning on and off rapidly, until evenly chopped. Correct amount of mayonnaise, if necessary, adding enough to bind. Turn on and off 2 or 3 times.

Perla Meyers' Tuna Pâté

10 ounces canned tuna
  in olive oil, drained
1 cup softened butter,
  cut in 6 pieces
2 to 3 drops lemon
  juice
2 to 3 drops Tabasco
Salt and freshly
  ground black
  pepper
10 medium shrimp,
  cooked and shelled
3 tablespoons coarsely
  chopped pimientos
2 tablespoons tiny
  capers, drained
Parsley sprigs
Buttered toast rounds

With the metal blade in place, add the tuna, butter, lemon juice, Tabasco, salt and pepper to the beaker. Process until the mixture is smooth. Add shrimp, pimientos and capers. Process, turning on and off rapidly, until ingredients are evenly chopped and combined. Taste and adjust seasoning; it must be highly seasoned. Pack the pâté into a well-oiled 3-cup loaf pan or mold and chill for 24 hours. Unmold onto a serving plate. Garnish with parsley and serve with toast rounds. Makes 3 cups.

Variations: The pâté can be made with crabmeat instead of shrimp or a combination of shrimp and crabmeat. It can also be flavored with fresh, finely minced dill or tarragon and a large pinch of curry.

Strathboro Paste

Strathboro Paste, a marvelous addition to an hors d'oeuvre table, goes beautifully with drinks. It should be served with a variety of cocktail breads.

2 cups cubed (1-inch pieces) well-done cooked beef
8 to 10 anchovy fillets
1 small onion, cut in 4 pieces
2 teaspoons sliced garlic
1 teaspoon crushed thyme
1 bay leaf, crumbled
Salt and pepper to taste
½ cup softened butter, cut in 4 pieces
Melted butter

With the metal blade in place, add the beef, anchovy fillets, onion, garlic, thyme, bay leaf, salt and pepper to beaker. Process, turning on and off rapidly until evenly chopped, about 8 to 10 seconds. Add the softened butter and continue processing until mixture is smooth. If additional butter is needed, add 1 tablespoon at a time. Transfer to a serving bowl. Pour melted butter over top to form a thin layer. If properly sealed with butter and refrigerated, the paste will keep for up to 3 weeks. Makes about 2¼ cups.

Onion Brioche Sandwiches

1 Brioche Loaf* (page 71)
Mayonnaise (page 67)
3 or 4 small white onions, peeled and sliced paper-thin
Salt
1½ to 2 cups chopped parsley

Slice brioche rather thin (bake it a day ahead to make slicing easier) and cut each slice into a round with a 2-inch cutter. Spread each round generously with mayonnaise. Place an onion slice on each of half the rounds, sprinkle lightly with salt and top with remaining rounds. Press together firmly and don't be dismayed if some of the mayonnaise is squeezed out.

Place a shallow plate of mayonnaise and one of chopped parsley side by side. Holding each sandwich between thumb and forefinger, roll edges first in mayonnaise, then in parsley to make a green wreath. Arrange the sandwiches on a plate, cover with plastic wrap and chill for about 1 hour before serving. Yield: See note.

*This brioche loaf will yield about 32 slices, each ¼-inch thick. Depending on how well your loaf rises, each slice will provide 1 or 2 rounds 2 inches in diameter, to make 16 or 32 sandwiches.

Craig Claiborne's and Pierre Franey's Mousseline of Chicken Livers

¾ cup pure chicken fat *
2 medium onions, quartered
2 medium garlic cloves
½ pound lean boneless veal, cut in 1-inch cubes
¼ teaspoon nutmeg
Salt and pepper to taste
1 pound clean chicken livers
½ bay leaf
2 sprigs fresh thyme *or*
½ teaspoon dried thyme leaves
3 tablespoons Cognac
¼ cup heavy cream
¼ cup chopped pistachio nuts
Buttered French bread toast

Melt chicken fat over moderate heat in large skillet. Meanwhile, with slicing disk in place, cover the beaker and stand the onion quarters upright in the feed tube. Slice, using moderate pressure on pusher. Add sliced onions to melted chicken fat and cook, stirring, until wilted. With the metal blade in place, add garlic to the beaker. Process until finely chopped. Add the veal, nutmeg, salt and pepper to onions. Cook about 2 minutes, stirring. Add chicken livers, chopped garlic, bay leaf and thyme. Cook, stirring occasionally, for about 5 minutes.

Remove bay leaf and thyme sprigs, if used. With metal blade in place, spoon mixture into beaker of food processor and add Cognac. Process, turning on and off rapidly for 10 seconds, then process for 30 seconds more or until smooth. Transfer to a mixing bowl and let cool to room temperature. Whip cream until stiff, then fold it into chicken liver mixture. Spoon into a decorative 5 to 6-cup mold. Chill well.

Serve, sprinkled with pistachio nuts, directly from the mold with buttered toast. Or, if desired, using 2 spoons, shape into oval "eggs". To do this, dip one spoon into hot water, then scoop up a portion of the mousseline. Dip other spoon in water and run inside first spoon and around the mousseline to shape the egg. Spoon portions onto plates and sprinkle each serving with pistachio nuts. Serve with buttered toast. Makes about 5 cups.

Variation: This mousseline may be made firm and unmolded, if 1 envelope softened gelatin is added to the hot chicken mixture as it is being puréed and the heavy cream is increased to ½ cup.

*Rendered chicken fat may be purchased in some supermarkets, or you can prepare it yourself. Cook scraps of chicken fat in a skillet over moderate heat until melted, or in 2 roasting pans in a 300 degree oven.

Spreads&Butters

Tuna Spread

1 **7-oz. can tuna, drained**
⅓ **cup mayonnaise (page 67)**
2 **parsley sprigs**
1 **green onion, cut in 1-inch pieces**
 Juice of ½ lemon
 Salt and pepper to taste
3 **or 4 anchovy fillets (optional)**

With the metal blade in place, add tuna, mayonnaise, parsley, onion, lemon juice, salt and pepper to the beaker. Process, turning on and off rapidly, until evenly mixed, about 8 to 10 seconds. Taste for additional salt and pepper. If anchovy fillets are used, process them first for a few seconds before adding other ingredients. Makes about 1 cup.

Brandade

This is one of the few dishes that doesn't taste at all as it reads. People have been known to become addicted to it and in France it is often served with a truffle garnish. It is a versatile dish and equally often, it is spread on toast, sprinkled with grated Swiss cheese and run briefly under the broiler. Brandade also can be mixed with cream puff dough and fried in deep fat for extremely good fritters.

1 **pound salt cod**
1 **garlic clove**
⅓ **cup olive oil**
3 **tablespoons heavy cream**

Soak cod overnight, changing the water twice. In the morning, rinse cod and cover with cold water. Bring to a boil, reduce heat and simmer until fish is tender, about 10 to 15 minutes. Drain and flake fish, removing sinews and bones. With the metal blade in place, add ½ the cod and garlic to the beaker. Process, turning on and off continuously, for about 30 seconds. Scrape down with a spatula and add remaining cod. Process again, turning on and off continuously, until evenly chopped, about 30 seconds. With machine running, gradually pour olive oil and cream through the feed tube. Process until completely smooth.

If brandade is refrigerated, it may thicken. If this happens, return it to beaker and pour in a little cream. Reheat in a thick-bottomed saucepan, stirring frequently. The spread should have the consistency of mashed potatoes. Makes about 2½ cups.

Leon Lianide's Tarama Salata

This spread is perfectly delicious when accompanied by toast points or celery.

1 **medium onion, quartered**
1 **garlic clove**
1 **parsley sprig**
1 **cup (8 ounces) tarama***
8 **slices firm white bread, soaked in water and squeezed dry**
1 **cup light olive oil**
  Juice of 3 lemons
3 **Greek black olives**
1 **small lemon, sliced**
1½ **tablespoons pistachio nuts, chopped**

With metal blade in place, add onion, garlic and parsley to the beaker. Process, turning on and off, until onion is evenly chopped. Add tarama and bread. Process until evenly mixed, about 10 seconds. Continue processing and slowly drizzle the olive oil and lemon juice through the feed tube.

Transfer to a serving dish. Chill at least 2 hours. Garnish with black olives and thin slices of lemon sprinkled with chopped pistachio nuts. The lemon can be sliced in the food processor using the slicing disk and the nuts can be chopped using the metal blade. Keep refrigerated until ready to serve. Makes about 3½ cups.

*Tarama is mullet roe from Greece. It is available at specialty food markets.

Cheese Spread

8 ounces gorganzola
  cheese, cut in
  pieces
4 ounces camembert
  cheese, cut in
  pieces
½ cup sweet butter, cut
  in pieces
¼ cup brandy

Let cheeses and butter warm to room temperature. With the metal blade in place, add cheeses, butter and brandy to beaker of food processor. Process, turning on and off continuously, for about 20 seconds. Then continue processing until a smooth spread is formed, about 20 seconds. Makes about 2 cups.

Chicken Liver and Avocado Spread

This is very much like a chicken liver terrine. It is wonderful as a first course or it can be served with toast or crackers as an hors d'oeuvre.

1 pound chicken
  livers
¼ cup butter
1 large avocado,
  peeled and cut in
  8 pieces (about
  1½ cups)
6 to 8 scallions (white
  part only), cut in
  1-inch pieces
¼ cup brandy
½ cup softened butter,
  cut in pieces
1½ teaspoons salt
1/8 teaspoon freshly
  ground black
  pepper

Sauté chicken livers in the ¼ cup butter over medium-high heat until livers are brown on outside but still red and juicy inside. With the metal blade in place, add the chicken livers, avocado, scallions and brandy to beaker. Process, turning on and off rapidly, until a smooth paste is formed, about 15 seconds. Add softened butter, salt and pepper. Process again until well mixed.

Transfer spread to a serving bowl. Place plastic wrap directly on spread to prevent discoloring. Cover bowl with additional plastic wrap to make an airtight seal. Refrigerate until needed. If you prefer, pack spread into a mold, then unmold at serving time. Makes about 3 cups.

Middle East Dip

1 4-oz. jar tarama*
1 15-oz. can chick peas,
  drained
4 green onions (white
  part only), cut in
  1-inch lengths
  Juice of 1 lemon
  (2 tablespoons)
2 garlic cloves

With the metal blade in place, add the tarama, chick peas, green onions, lemon juice and garlic to the beaker. Process, turning on and off rapidly, for 10 seconds. Continue processing until a smooth dip is formed, about 15 seconds. Makes about 2½ cups.

*Tarama is fish roe from Greece and Turkey. It is available at specialty food markets.

Anchoiade Nicoise

This appetizer spread from Provence in Southern France will make a welcome new addition to your hors d'oeuvre list. It should be served on melba toast or toast points spread with garlic butter.

2/3 cup toasted filbert nuts
1 cup dried figs, stemmed and quartered
1 2-oz. can anchovy fillets with oil
3 garlic cloves
1/4 cup olive oil

With the metal blade in place, add the filberts to beaker. Process until finely chopped. Without removing nuts, add figs, anchovies with oil and garlic. Process, turning on and off, until very finely chopped and beginning to purée. Continue processing and slowly add oil through feed tube to make a smooth paste. Makes about 1 1/2 cups.

Deviled Ham

2 cups diced cooked ham (about 3/4 pound)
2 tablespoons mayonnaise
1 1/2 tablespoons Dijon mustard
1/4 teaspoon Tabasco

With the metal blade in place, add ham to beaker of food processor. Process, turning on and off rapidly, until a smooth paste is formed. Add mayonnaise, mustard and Tabasco. Process until blended. Makes about 1 1/2 cups.

Variations: 1) To ham mixture, add 5 small sweet mustard pickles, 1 tablespoon mayonnaise and 1 tablespoon hot mustard. 2) Add 1/2 cup dry roasted or unsalted peanuts, 2 tablespoons Dijon mustard, 1 tablespoon mayonnaise and 3 tablespoons Madeira wine. Proceed as before, processing until pickles or nuts are evenly chopped.

Guacamole

4 medium-sized ripe avocadoes, peeled and cut in pieces
1/2 small onion, cut in pieces
2 canned, peeled green chili peppers, seeded
Juice of 2 lemons (1/4 cup)
2 garlic cloves
1 teaspoon salt
1/4 teaspoon pepper

With the metal blade in place, add the avocado, onion, green chilies, lemon juice, garlic, salt and pepper to the beaker of the food processor. Process, turning on and off rapidly, until desired texture is reached. Do not process until smooth. Guacamole should have small chunks of avocado and onion in it. Taste and adjust seasoning. Makes about 2 cups.

Variations: To basic recipe, add any of the following: 1 to 2 teaspoons chili powder, 1/2 cup crisply-fried, crumbled bacon, 1/2 cup finely chopped nuts or 1/2 cup tiny cooked Pacific or bay shrimp. Chop nuts or shrimp before making guacamole, then stir in just before serving.

Roquefort Paste

8 ounces Roquefort
   cheese, cut in
   pieces
1 8-oz. package cream
   cheese, cut in
   pieces
½ cup butter, cut in
   pieces
1 garlic clove
3 tablespoons Cognac

Let cheeses and butter warm to room temperature. With metal blade in place, add garlic and Roquefort cheese to beaker of food processor. Process, turning on and off rapidly, until garlic is chopped and evenly distributed, about 10 seconds. Add cream cheese, butter and Cognac. Continue processing until a smooth paste is formed. Makes about 2 cups.

Peanut Butter

To the beaker of the machine equipped with the metal blade, add 1 or 2 cups of cocktail peanuts. Put pusher in cover and start processing. Wait until peanuts form a ball which will spin briefly around the beaker before disappearing (about 90 seconds). Remove cover and scrape down. Replace cover and run 15 seconds more. Taste and add salt, if desired. If the spread seems too stiff or too dry, continue processing until desired consistency is reached.

Cashew Butter

Use in sauces, fillings, frostings or as you would use peanut butter.

2 cups (about 12
   ounces) cashews
2 tablespoons butter
½ to 1 teaspoon salt

With the metal blade in place, add cashews to the beaker of the food processor. Process, turning on and off rapidly, until cashews are very finely ground and have begun to crawl up the side of the beaker. Add butter and continue processing until smooth. Taste and add salt as needed. Process for a few seconds and taste again. Makes about 1 cup.

Herb Butter

¼ cup loosely packed
   mint leaves
¼ cup loosely packed
   chives
¼ cup loosely packed
   parsley
1 cup butter, cut in
   pieces

With the metal blade in place, add mint leaves, chives and parsley to the beaker. Process, turning on and off, until greens are finely chopped. Add butter. Process again, turning on and off, scraping sides as necessary, to make a smooth butter. This should take about 30 to 40 seconds. Makes about 1 cup.

Almond Butter

Use as a spread for sandwiches or to flavor frostings and cake fillings.

2 cups (about 12 ounces) whole, blanched almonds
¼ cup butter, cut in pieces
½ teaspoon almond extract

With the metal blade in place, add almonds to the beaker. Process, turning on and off rapidly, until almonds are very finely ground and have begun to crawl up the side of the beaker. Add butter and almond extract through feed tube and continue processing until smooth. Makes about 1¼ cups.

Snail Butter

Delicious, not only in the classical escargot preparation, but also as a filling for broiled mushroom caps.

¼ cup loosely packed parsley sprigs
1 small shallot
1 garlic clove
2 tablespoons white wine
1 cup butter, cut in pieces

With the metal blade in place, add parsley, shallot, garlic and wine to the beaker. Process, turning on and off rapidly, until finely chopped. Add butter and process, turning on and off, until smooth. If necessary, stop processing and scrape mixture from sides with spatula. Makes about 1 cup.

Crunchy Peanut Spread

3 cups (about 16 ounces) peanuts, shelled, skinned and salted
4 tablespoons peanut oil
1 to 2 teaspoons salt, depending on saltiness of nuts

With the metal blade in place, add peanuts to the beaker. Process, turning on and off rapidly until peanuts are finely ground and begin to climb the side of the beaker, about 15 seconds. Add oil through feed tube and process about 15 seconds. Taste for salt, adding as much as needed. Process for 5 seconds and taste again. Makes about 2 cups.

Soups

Pumpkin Soup

This is a wonderful winter soup, especially good when garnished with sour cream and sprinkled with parsley and cinnamon.

1 large onion, halved
¼ cup butter
½ teaspoon curry powder
2 cups canned pumpkin
1½ teaspoons salt
2 cups heavy cream
2½ cups chicken stock

With the slicing disk in place, slice onion using moderate pressure on pusher of food processor. Melt the butter in a skillet, add the onion and sauté until limp. Sprinkle with curry powder and sauté an additional minute or two. With the metal blade in place, add curried onions, pumpkin and salt to the beaker. Process until mixed, about 10 seconds, then quickly pour in heavy cream while continuing to process. Transfer pumpkin purée to a large saucepan and heat slowly with chicken stock. Garnish and serve steaming hot. Makes about 1½ quarts.

Carrot Vichyssoise

2 large carrots, peeled
and cut in pieces
2 medium potatoes,
peeled and cubed
1 leek (white part only),
cut in pieces
3 cups chicken stock
1 cup heavy cream
Salt and pepper to
taste
Chopped chives

With the metal blade in place, add the carrots, potatoes and leek to the beaker. Process, turning on and off rapidly, until coarsely chopped, about 15 to 20 seconds. In large saucepan, combine chopped vegetables with chicken stock and simmer for 30 minutes. Strain vegetables, allowing liquid to drain into a storage container. Reinsert metal blade and purée vegetable mixture in 2 batches. Combine batches with vegetable liquid. Stir in cream. Season with slightly more salt and pepper than necessary as the taste will be dulled when the soup is chilled. Cover and refrigerate. Serve very cold, garnished with chives. Makes about 4 cups.

Variations: 1) Add 1 large bunch watercress leaves to vegetable mixture just before cooking for Watercress Vichyssoise.   2) For Apple Vichyssoise, add ½ cup chopped raw apple to vegetable mixture before cooling.

Cucumber Soup

1 small onion, whole
or halved
2 cups plain yogurt
2 teaspoons white
vinegar
2 teaspoons olive oil
12 to 15 fresh mint
leaves or
½ teaspoons dried
mint leaves
1 garlic clove
1 teaspoon salt
½ teaspoon dried dill
weed
1 cucumber, peeled
and seeded

With the shredding disk in place, shred onion. Replace shredding disk with metal blade and add yogurt, vinegar, olive oil, mint leaves, garlic, salt and dill weed to the beaker. Process until a smooth mixture is formed, about 15 to 20 seconds. Remove chopping blade, disturbing yogurt mixture as little as possible, and reinsert shredding disk. Cover and fit cucumber into the feed tube. Shred, using moderate pressure on plunger. Transfer* the soup to a bowl. Cover and chill. Serve very cold. If desired, top each serving with freshly chopped dill or parsley. Makes about 2 cups.

*Remember—never remove cover until motor stops!

Barbara Kafka's Gazpacho

There are as many variations for this substantial summer soup as there are Spaniards. One thing is clear, however, real Gazpacho bears no resemblance to the homogenous liquid served in most restaurants. It was always made by finely hand chopping the ingredients. Therefore, it is unnecessary—though pretty—to serve side bowls of chopped ingredients. Properly made, the Gazpacho will have a wonderful texture of its own.

Preparation of the ingredients has always been a time consuming task; now, with the food processor, it is very quick. Do make the soup a few hours ahead so that it has time for the flavors to combine and to chill. Even if nothing special is planned, it is fun to have a jar in the refrigerator. You will be surprised how quickly it will disappear.

½ Bermuda or other sweet white onion, peeled and quartered

1½ firm medium cucumbers, peeled and cut in pieces

2 small sweet green peppers, seeded and cut in eighths

6 medium to large tomatoes, peeled and cut in eighths

5 large garlic cloves

1 cup (or more) tomato juice

½ cup light olive oil

¾ teaspoon chili powder or

1 small piece fresh chili pepper

1 tablespoon kosher salt

With the metal blade in place, add the onion to the beaker. Process, turning on and off rapidly, until finely chopped, about 4 or 5 seconds. Transfer onion to a large bowl. Repeat with cucumbers, then with green peppers, adding each to bowl with onions. Process 5 of the tomatoes until evenly chopped into small pieces. Transfer to bowl with other chopped ingredients. Process remaining tomato with garlic, tomato juice, olive oil and chili powder until a smooth liquid is formed. Combine with chopped vegetables and chill in a covered container. Before serving, taste for salt. If texture is too thick, add more tomato juice or a combination of ½ tomato juice and ½ beef bouillon. Makes about 1½ quarts.

Note: Vegetables are chopped separately to enable control of the texture of each. It is not necessary to wash beaker of processor between vegetables.

Vichyssoise

2 leeks, cut in pieces
1 small onion,
   quartered
¼ cup butter
3 large potatoes,
   peeled and cut in
   1-inch pieces
6 cups chicken stock
2 teaspoons salt
½ teaspoon pepper
2 cups heavy cream
   Chopped chives

With the metal blade in place, add the leeks and onion to the beaker. Process, turning on and off rapidly, until evenly chopped, about 4 or 5 seconds. Sauté leeks and onions in butter until tender. Transfer to a large soup kettle and add potatoes, chicken stock, salt and pepper. Bring to a boil, then reduce heat and simmer, covered, until potatoes are tender. Strain vegetables, allowing liquid to drain into a storage container. With the metal blade in place, add ½ the cooked, drained vegetables to the beaker and process until smooth. Continue processing and pour ½ the cream through feed tube. Transfer to storage container with liquid. Repeat with remaining vegetables and cream. Cover and chill until ready to serve. Serve garnished with chopped chives. Makes about 2 quarts.

Lentil Soup

Serve the soup steaming hot on a cold winter day or, during the summer, serve it chilled with a dollop of sour cream and a sprinkling of chopped parsley.

2 cups dry lentils
2½ quarts water
2 to 3 pounds veal
   knuckles
2 carrots, cut in
   pieces
1 large onion,
   quartered
1 celery rib, cut in
   pieces
1 garlic clove
2 bay leaves
1 tablespoon crushed
   thyme
1 tablespoon salt
½ teaspoon freshly
   ground black pepper
½ to ¾ pound smoked
   sausage

In large kettle, combine lentils, water, veal knuckles, carrots, onion, celery, garlic, bay leaves, thyme, salt and pepper. Bring to boil, reduce heat and simmer, covered, until lentils are soft and tender, about 2 hours. Strain, reserving liquid. Discard bones.
   With the metal blade in place, add ⅓ lentil mixture to the beaker and process until puréed, about 5 seconds. Pour into reserved liquid. Repeat twice, using ½ remaining lentil mixture each time. With the slicing disk in place, slice sausage using moderate pressure on the pusher. Add sausage to puréed soup. Place over low heat and simmer, covered, for 30 to 45 minutes. Makes about 3 quarts.

Andre Soltner's Onion Soup

1 **large or 2 medium onions, cut in eighths (about 10 ounces)**
1 **tablespoon butter**
½ **tablespoon flour**
1 **cup dry white wine**
8 **cups chicken stock**
Salt and pepper to taste
2 **ounces Swiss cheese, cut to fit feed tube of processor**
French bread croutons (oven-toasted slices about ½-inch thick)

With the metal blade in place, add the onion to the beaker of food processor. Process, turning on and off rapidly, until onion is coarsely chopped, about 4 or 5 seconds. Cook onion in butter until golden brown. Add flour and stir until blended. Gradually stir in wine and chicken stock. Season with salt and pepper. Bring to boil, then reduce heat and boil gently for 45 minutes.

Meanwhile, with the shredding disk in place, shred cheese, using moderate pressure on the pusher. Just before serving, sauté croutons in additional butter. Ladle soup into bowls and top each with a crouton. Sprinkle with cheese and place under broiler until cheese is melted and lightly browned. Serve steaming hot. Makes about 7 cups.

Zucchini Bisque

1 **medium onion, quartered**
½ **cup butter**
1½ **pounds zucchini**
2½ **cups chicken stock**
½ **teaspoon nutmeg**
1 **teaspoon basil**
1 **teaspoon salt**
Freshly ground black pepper
1 **cup heavy cream**

With the metal blade in place, add the onion to the beaker of the food processor. Process, turning on and off rapidly, until evenly chopped, about 5 seconds. In large saucepan, melt the butter. Add onion and sauté until limp. With shredding disk in place, shred zucchini using moderate pressure on the pusher. Add zucchini and chicken stock to the onion. Simmer, covered, for 15 minutes. Reinsert metal blade and purée zucchini mixture in processor in 2 batches, adding ½ the nutmeg, basil, salt and a few grinds of pepper to each. Combine batches, add cream and stir until well mixed. Taste for additional seasoning. Serve hot or cold. Makes about 1 ½ quarts.

Soupe de Poisson Marseillaise

2 medium onions, quartered
2 large leeks (white part only), cut in pieces
4 or 5 tablespoons olive oil
6 garlic cloves
2 tomatoes, peeled, seeded and quartered
3 quarts water
2 pounds sole fillets, cut in thirds
  Fish heads, scraps and bones (tied in a cheesecloth bag)
3 tablespoons Cognac
½ pound orzo*
  Salt and pepper to taste
2 large pinches saffron threads, if possible, pounded in a mortar and pestle with the salt
  Parmesan cheese
  Garlic croutons
  Rouille (recipe follows)

With the metal blade in place, add onions and leeks to the beaker. Process, turning on and off, until finely chopped, about 5 seconds. Heat olive oil in a large saucepan, add onions and leeks and cook over low to moderate heat until tender. With metal blade in place, add garlic to the beaker. Process until finely chopped. Add tomatoes and process, turning on and off twice, or until evenly chopped.

Pour into the saucepan with the onions and leeks and cook 1 minute. Add water, sole and the bag of fish heads, scraps and bones. Simmer for 20 minutes. Drain, reserving liquid. Remove cheesecloth bag and discard.

With the metal blade in place, add vegetables and fish to the beaker of the food processor. Process, turning on and off, until puréed, about 10 seconds. Return to saucepan with reserved liquid. Bring to boil and add Cognac and orzo. Season with salt, pepper and saffron. Cook gently until pasta is soft. Serve with grated Parmesan cheese, garlic croutons and rouille. Makes about 3½ quarts.

*Orzo is a rice-shaped pasta often used in soups. It is available in many supermarkets.

Rouille

A rouille is a fiery hot French sauce from Provence. It should be passed at the table and stirred into the soup. While the rouille aficionado may add 2 or 3 tablespoons, the uninitiated should start with a teaspoon or two.

8 garlic cloves
3 small dried red peppers
½ slice white bread, crust removed
¼ cup olive oil
2 tablespoons tomato paste
1 teaspoon paprika
4 to 5 drops Tabasco
½ cup fish stock

With the metal blade in place, add the garlic, red peppers, bread, olive oil, tomato paste, paprika, Tabasco and fish stock to the beaker of food processor. Process, turning on and off, for about 5 seconds, then continue processing for an additional 10 seconds to make a smooth paste, adding more fish stock if necessary. For a hotter rouille, add more Tabasco. Serve with Soupe de Poisson Marseillaise.

Main Courses

Meatballs

½ **pound boneless
  lean beef, cut in
  1-inch cubes**
1 **pound boneless
  veal, cut in 1-inch
  cubes**
½ **pound boneless
  lean pork, cut in
  1-inch cubes**
1 **large onion,
  quartered**
1 **slice white bread,
  cut in pieces**
1 **egg**
1½ **teaspoons salt**
½ **teaspoon pepper**
1 **teaspoon crushed
  thyme leaves**
¼ **teaspoon grated
  nutmeg**
2 **tablespoons olive oil
  Basic Tomato Sauce
  (page 63)**

With the metal blade in place, add the beef to the
beaker. Process, turning on and off rapidly, until
meat is evenly and finely chopped, about
5 seconds. Transfer to a large bowl. Repeat 3 times
with veal and pork, processing ½ pound meat each
time. Add the onion, bread, egg, salt, pepper,
thyme and nutmeg to beaker. Process, turning on
and off rapidly until almost smooth, about
10 seconds. Stir into meat mixture and form into small
balls. Heat olive oil in large skillet. Add meatballs
and brown on all sides. Transfer to a casserole, add
Basic Tomato Sauce and place in preheated
350 degree oven until heated, about 20 minutes.

Variation: Omit tomato sauce and deglaze skillet
with 1 cup beef stock and 2 tablespoons tomato
paste. Return meatballs to skillet and simmer
15 minutes. Meatballs may be stored several hours or
overnight in a covered container in refrigerator. To
reheat, return to skillet and simmer but do not boil
until meatballs are heated through, then gently stir
in 1 cup of sour cream. Makes about 50 meatballs,
1¼ inches in diameter.

Craig Claiborne's and Pierre Franey's Mousse of Shrimp with Sauce Joinville

¾ pound raw, shelled, deveined shrimp
½ teaspoon salt
1/8 teaspoon nutmeg
1/8 teaspoon cayenne pepper
Freshly ground black pepper to taste
1 egg
1¼ cups heavy cream
Sauce Joinville (recipe follows)

With the metal blade in place, add the shrimp, salt, nutmeg and peppers to the beaker of food processor. Process, turning on and off rapidly, until shrimp are finely chopped, about 30 seconds. Scrape down with a spatula, if necessary. Add the egg and process until mixture is smooth, about 20 seconds. Continue processing and slowly add cream. Process about 30 seconds. Mixture will be thick and smooth. To taste for seasoning, drop a small spoonful of the mixture into a saucepan with boiling water. Cook briefly and taste. Add more seasoning if desired.

Spoon mixture into a well-buttered 3-cup mold. Cover with a buttered round of wax paper cut to fit top of mousse. Place mold in shallow baking pan on oven shelf. Pour in boiling water to depth ½ way up sides of mold. Bake in preheated 375 degree oven 30 to 40 minutes or until a long needle inserted in center of mousse comes out clean. Do not overbake. Unmold mousse onto a serving plate. If any liquid seeps from mousse, drain it off. Dribble some of the Sauce Joinville over the mousse and serve remaining sauce on the side. Makes 4 to 6 servings.

Sauce Joinville

4 tablespoons butter
2 tablespoons flour
1 cup fish stock (page 31)
½ cup heavy cream
1 egg yolk
5 large shallots
¼ pound mushrooms
¼ pound raw, shelled, deveined shrimp, cut in ½-inch pieces
Salt and pepper to taste
2 tablespoons dry white wine
1½ teaspoons lemon juice

Melt 2 tablespoons of the butter in a saucepan and add flour, stirring with wire whisk. When blended, add fish stock, stirring rapidly. When smooth, continue to cook, stirring frequently, for about 20 minutes. Mix the cream with the egg yolk. Add mixture to the fish stock, stirring rapidly with whisk, until it reaches the boil. Swirl in 1 tablespoon butter. Remove from heat. While sauce is being prepared, with the metal blade in place, add the shallots to the beaker. Process until finely chopped. Sauté in 1 tablespoon butter. With slicing disk in place, cover and fill the feed tube with the mushrooms, standing them on edge. Slice, using steady moderate pressure on the pusher.

Add the mushroom slices to the saucepan with the shallots. Cook, stirring, until mushrooms are limp, about 5 minutes. Add shrimp, salt and pepper to the mushroom-shallot mixture. Cook, stirring occasionally, about 1 minute. Add the wine and continue cooking, stirring occasionally, about 5 minutes. Stir into sauce and bring just to the boil. Taste and adjust seasonings. Add lemon juice and serve with Mousse of Shrimp. Makes about 1½ cups.

Jacques Pépin's Quenelles Galliera

The light, delicately-flavored fish dumplings called quenelles are a highlight of French haute cuisine, and those made in Jacques Pépin's native Lyonnais region are the best in France. In this dish, they are presented with a seafood-mushroom sauce.

For convenience, the recipe is divided into parts. The quenelles, the fish stock or the velouté sauce and the duxelles can be prepared in advance.

Quenelles Lyonnaises

⅔ **cup milk**
1½ **to 2 teaspoons salt**
1/8 **to ¼ teaspoon freshly grated nutmeg**
3 **ounces (¾ stick) sweet butter**
3⅓ **ounces all-purpose flour (see note at bottom of page for measuring flour if scale is not available)**
2 **large eggs**
3 **ounces (¾ stick) sweet butter at room temperature**
10 **ounces boneless pike, flounder or halibut (1 tightly packed 8-ounce measure)**

For panade, combine milk, salt, nutmeg and 3 ounces butter in a saucepan. Bring to boil slowly (butter must melt). Add flour all at once and stir vigorously until thoroughly mixed. Transfer to a plate or tray and flatten. Cover with plastic wrap and refrigerate until chilled.

With metal blade in place, add panade, cut in 1-inch pieces, and eggs to beaker of food processor. Process 10 seconds. Add 3 ounces room temperature butter and process until smooth. Add fish. Process 5 seconds on, 5 seconds off until perfectly smooth. Poach a teaspoon of mixture in boiling water until puffed. Taste and correct seasoning. Refrigerate covered.

To shape quenelles, prepare a well-floured board with a small heap of flour in one corner. Line a ¼-cup measure with plastic wrap and pack with well-chilled quenelle mixture. Unmold on heap of flour. Remove plastic wrap and with floured hand roll into a 3-inch long cylinder. Pat ends flat. Roll onto a spatula and transfer to a baking pan. Repeat until all the mixture is shaped. Refrigerate covered until chilled (up to 24 hours).

To poach, place quenelles in single layer in a well-buttered 12-inch straight-sided skillet. Fill with boiling salted water to within ½ inch above quenelles. Poach over low heat (160 to 180°F.) for 20 minutes, turning once. If water temperature exceeds 180°F., quenelles will not puff properly during final cooking. Remove with a skimmer and place in cold water. When cold, refrigerate in covered container up to 24 hours before final use. Makes 13 to 15 quenelles, 2 ounces each.

Note: Spoon flour into a 1-cup liquid measure and shake gently sideways to level flour. For 3⅓ ounces flour, add enough flour to measure ⅔ cup.

Fish Stock

1 large onion,
  quartered
2 tablespoons sweet
  butter
2 pounds fish bones
  (flat fish like sole are
  best; avoid heads;
  and be sure to clean
  gills or stock will be
  bitter)
10 sprigs parsley
1 teaspoon white
  peppercorns
½ teaspoon crushed
  thyme leaves
2 bay leaves
1 teaspoon salt
1 cup dry white wine
4 cups water

With the slicing disk in place, add the onion to the beaker of food processor. Slice, using moderate pressure on pusher. Melt butter in large pot (not aluminum). Add bones and cook, stirring, over medium heat for 1 minute. Add all other ingredients except the wine and water. Stir until mixed. Cover and cook over medium heat for 3 or 4 minutes. Add the wine and water. Bring to boil and let boil gently for 20 minutes. Strain through a fine sieve. The stock may be frozen for future use.

Velouté Sauce

5 tablespoons butter
¾ cup all-purpose flour
4 cups fish stock

Melt butter in a heavy saucepan. Stir in the flour and cook over low heat for 1 minute, stirring constantly with a whisk. Add fish stock and bring to boil, stirring to prevent scorching. Let cook over low heat for 30 minutes, stirring occasionally. The sauce can be frozen or kept for up to 2 weeks in a covered container in the refrigerator.

Duxelles

1 pound mushrooms,
  cut in pieces
5 shallots, peeled
3 tablespoons sweet
  butter
½ teaspoon salt
¼ teaspoon freshly
  ground white pepper

With the metal blade in place, add 6 to 8 mushrooms at a time to the beaker, making sure that the beaker is never more than half filled. Process, turning on and off rapidly, until mushrooms are finely chopped, about 8 to 10 seconds. Transfer to a large bowl and repeat until all the mushrooms are chopped. Place mushrooms in a kitchen towel and squeeze out all the liquid. (You can save the liquid for flavoring sauces or for use in vegetable stock.)

Add shallots to the beaker and process until finely chopped. Melt the butter in a skillet. Add the shallots and cook over medium heat for 1 minute. Add the chopped mushrooms, salt and pepper. Cook very slowly, stirring occasionally, until liquid disappears and mixture is dry. Transfer to a bowl, cover with plastic wrap and set aside.

Final Assembly

2 cups heavy cream
1 cup milk
2½ cups Velouté Sauce
   Duxelles
1 tablespoon Cognac
13 to 15 Quenelles
   Lyonnaises

Combine the cream, milk, Velouté Sauce, Duxelles, and Cognac in a large, flat saucepan with a cover*. Bring to boil, stirring with a whisk. Add quenelles (they should fit without overlapping), cover and simmer for 25 minutes, shaking the pan every 5 minutes to move the quenelles and prevent them from sticking. It is best to place the pan on an asbestos pad. The quenelles should almost double in volume. Serve them hot, 1 or 2 per person with a few tablespoons of sauce

*Select a pan that is nice enough to bring to the dining table. It may be necessary to use two pans.

Chicken in Lettuce Leaves

¾ cup natural whole
   almonds
   Water
1 cup loosely packed
   parsley sprigs
4 medium onions
1 medium green
   pepper
6 tablespoons butter
1 fresh hot red pepper,
   seeded and cut in
   thirds
2 or 3 fresh basil
   leaves or
1½ teaspoons dried
   basil leaves
4 cups cooked
   chicken, skin and
   bones removed and
   cubed
1 teaspoon salt
½ teaspoon freshly
   ground black pepper
⅓ cup Cognac
½ cup chicken broth (if
   needed)
   Crisp iceberg
   lettuce leaves

Place almonds in a saucepan. Cover with water and simmer for 3 minutes. Drain, cool slightly and slip off skins. Toast in 350 degree oven for about 15 minutes. With the metal blade in place, add the parsley to the beaker. Process, turning on and off, until evenly chopped. Remove metal blade and insert slicing disk*. Slice almonds over parsley; remove and reserve for garnish.

Cut onions into lengthwise halves or quarters to fit feed tube. Cut ends from green pepper and remove seeds. If too large to fit feed tube, cut lengthwise into halves. Reinsert slicing disk and slice first the onions, then the green pepper, using moderate pressure on the pusher. Sauté the onions and green pepper in the butter until wilted.

With the metal blade in place, combine the hot pepper, basil and ½ the chicken in the beaker. Process, turning on and off 4 or 5 times. Add the remaining chicken, onion and green pepper. Process, turning on and off, only until finely diced. Check frequently. Do not overprocess. Return to pan. Cover and simmer for 4 or 5 minutes. Add salt, pepper and Cognac. Taste and adjust seasoning. If more liquid is needed, add chicken broth.

Spoon into a mound on a heated serving platter. Sprinkle with parsley-almond mixture. Accompany with icy cold lettuce leaves. Let each person spoon some of the mixture on a lettuce leaf and roll it up. Makes about 4 cups.

*If you have the fine, serrated slicing disk, Part No. FP 731, use it to slice the almonds.

Turbans of Sole with Shrimp Mousse

1 pound raw, shelled, deveined shrimp
3 egg whites
1¼ cups heavy cream
½ teaspoon salt
¼ teaspoon pepper
¼ teaspoon freshly grated nutmeg
¼ teaspoon freshly chopped dill
6 sole fillets (about 1½ pounds)
White Wine Sauce (recipe follows)

With the metal blade in place, add the shrimp and egg whites to the beaker. Process, turning on and off, until a very smooth paste is formed, about 30 to 40 seconds. Continue processing and gradually pour the cream through the feed tube. Season with salt, pepper, nutmeg and dill. Cut fillets in pieces and line 6 buttered 6-ounce custard cups, reserving 6 pieces to cover tops.

Divide shrimp mixture among custard cups, putting about ½ cup in each. Cover with remaining sole pieces. Place the cups in a baking pan, add hot water to come ½ way up sides of cups and place in preheated 425 degree oven for 15 to 20 minutes. Remove from oven and invert cups onto dinner plates for serving. Serve with White Wine Sauce or chill and serve cold with mayonnaise made in the food processor (page 67). Makes 6 servings.

White Wine Sauce

4 tablespoons butter
3 tablespoons flour
½ cup fish broth (page 31)
1 cup milk
½ cup white wine
2 egg yolks
Salt and pepper to taste
Freshly grated nutmeg

Melt the butter in a saucepan. Blend in flour and cook until slightly colored. Stir in fish broth. When smooth, gradually add milk and continue cooking, stirring, until thickened. Add wine and egg yolks. Heat through, stirring constantly. Do not let sauce boil. Season with salt, pepper and nutmeg. Makes about 2 cups.

Saucisson en Brioche

2 cotechino or kielbasy sausages
Brioche Loaf (page 71)
1 egg yolk
2 tablespoons milk or cream

Poach sausages for 20 to 25 minutes in boiling water. When cool enough to handle, remove skin. Cool completely. Prepare brioche dough. After first rising, punch down and roll out to ⅓-inch thickness. Place sausages on dough and cut pieces large enough to wrap entire sausages in dough. Bring sides up around sausages, tucking in ends and pinching edges together to overlap. Place seam side down on buttered baking sheet. Cover and let rise in warm place for 10 minutes. Brush dough with an egg wash made by mixing egg yolk with milk or cream. Bake in preheated 375 degree oven for about 35 minutes or until brioche is baked and lightly browned. Slice and serve with hot potato salad and a variety of mustards.

Cheese Pudding

¾ **pound sharp Cheddar cheese, cut in pieces**
6 **slices white bread**
Butter
1½ **cups milk**
4 **eggs**
1 **teaspoon paprika**
½ **teaspoon salt**
¼ **teaspoon prepared mustard (or more)**

With the metal blade in place, add the cheese to the beaker. Process, turning on and off rapidly, until evenly chopped. Spread bread slices with butter and cut in pieces. Add the buttered bread, milk, eggs, paprika, salt and mustard to the cheese in the beaker. Process until thoroughly blended, about 30 seconds. Pour mixture into a buttered 2-quart casserole and bake in preheated 325 degree oven for 45 minutes or until pudding is set. Serve warm as a light entrée. Makes 4 servings.

Spinach Quiche

Pâte Brisée (page 75)
Uncooked beans or rice
Egg yolk, beaten
2 **pounds fresh spinach** *or* **2 10-oz. packages frozen spinach**
4 **ounces Gruyère or Swiss cheese, cut in 1-inch cubes**
3 **drops lemon juice**
1 **teaspoon salt**
¾ **teaspoon dried tarragon**
Dash of nutmeg
Dijon mustard
3 **eggs**
1½ **cups heavy cream** *or* ¾ **cup heavy cream and** ¾ **cup plain yogurt**

Use ½ the Pâte Brisée recipe. Roll out dough and line a 9-inch pie plate or tart pan (the kind with a removable bottom is good for quiche). Prick bottom and sides with a fork. Cover bottom with a round of waxed paper or foil and weight it down with about 2 cups uncooked beans or rice. Bake in a preheated 425 degree oven for 18 minutes. Remove beans or rice and the paper. Brush the pastry with a little beaten egg yolk and bake until lightly browned, about 3 minutes longer. Cool before filling.

Thoroughly wash fresh spinach and place in a heavy pan with no water except that clinging to the leaves. Cover and cook over medium to high heat only until wilted. If using frozen spinach, cook without salt according to package directions. Drain thoroughly, pressing down on spinach to extract all liquid.

With the metal blade in place, add cheese to beaker and process, turning on and off, until cheese is finely chopped. Remove and set aside. Reinsert metal blade and add drained spinach, lemon juice, salt, tarragon and nutmeg to beaker. Process until finely chopped.

Spread baked pie shell with mustard. Spoon spinach mixture evenly over the mustard and sprinkle top with the finely chopped cheese. Again, using the metal blade, process eggs and cream until thoroughly mixed.

Place pie on extended lower rack of oven. Pour egg-cream mixture over surface and gently push rack back into oven. Bake in a preheated 350 degree oven for 30 minutes or until set. Makes 4 to 6 main-course servings.

Helen McCully's Shad Roe Mousse with Sauce Mousseline

An elegant first course at an important dinner or the main course at luncheon.

Butter
2 pairs large *or*
 3 small shad roe
3 egg whites
1 cup heavy cream
Salt and freshly
 ground black
 pepper
Cayenne pepper
Dash of paprika
Parsley or dill sprigs
Sauce Mousseline*

Butter a 1½-quart soufflé dish thoroughly and refrigerate. Cut roes apart and remove as much of the filmy skin as possible and chop coarsely. With the metal blade in place, add the roe to the beaker of the food processor. Process until a smooth purée is formed. Add the egg whites, cream and seasonings to taste to the purée in the beaker. Process for 1 minute.

Pour into prepared mold, cover with waxed paper and refrigerate about 30 minutes. To bake, place mold in a baking pan. Add boiling water to reach ⅔ the depth of the mold. Bake in preheated 350 degree oven for 1¼ hours. To serve, unmold on a heated serving platter and garnish with parsley or dill. Makes 6 servings.

*Sauce Mousseline is a combination of Hollandaise and whipped heavy cream (2 parts Hollandaise to 1 part cream). To serve, place the whipped cream on top of the Hollandaise and allow guests to help themselves, plunging through the cream into the sauce which automatically mixes the two.

Chicken Hash

1 large onion,
 quartered
¼ cup butter
5 small cooked
 potatoes, peeled
⅛ teaspoon dried
 rosemary leaves
Salt and pepper to
 taste
2 cups coarsely
 chopped cooked
 chicken
2 chicken gizzards,
 halved
½ cup chicken stock
⅓ cup heavy cream
1 cup loosely packed
 parsley sprigs

With the metal blade in place, add the onion to the beaker. Process, turning on and off rapidly, until finely chopped. Sauté in melted butter until limp. Insert the slicing disk and slice potatoes, using moderate pressure on pusher. Add potato slices to the onions and season with rosemary, salt and pepper. Cook for 2 to 3 minutes, stirring gently. Using the metal blade, process chicken and chicken gizzards, each separately, until finely chopped. Add chopped chicken, gizzards and stock to potato-onion mixture. Cook over low heat for 5 minutes, then pour in cream and let cook until browned. Meanwhile, reinsert the metal blade and chop the parsley. Fold parsley into chicken mixture. Makes 4 to 6 servings.

Variations: 1) Add ½ cup finely chopped, sautéed mushrooms or toasted almonds, just before serving. 2) Omit the cream, stir in 2 egg yolks, sprinkle with grated Parmesan cheese and place under the broiler for a few minutes to set the egg and brown the cheese. Use the metal blade of food processor to chop the mushrooms, the slicing disk to slice the almonds and the metal blade to grate the cheese.

Spinach Roll with Shrimp Paste and Shrimp Sauce

Spinach Roll

1½ **slices dry bread, cut in pieces**
 2 **ounces Parmesan cheese, cut in pieces**
 3 **pounds fresh spinach *or* 3 10-ounce packages frozen spinach**
 6 **tablespoons butter, cut in pieces**
   Salt and pepper to taste
   Freshly grated nutmeg
 4 **eggs, separated**

With the metal blade in place, add the bread to the beaker. Process to make fine bread crumbs. Remove and reserve. Reinsert the metal blade, add cheese and process until very finely chopped. Remove and reserve. If using fresh spinach, wash well in lukewarm water and remove stems. Place in saucepan without water except that clinging to the leaves. Cover and cook until wilted. Drain well, pressing out all excess liquid. If using frozen spinach, thaw over low heat and drain thoroughly. With the metal blade in place, add the spinach to the beaker and process until finely chopped. Add the butter, salt, pepper and nutmeg. Continue processing until smooth, adding the egg yolks one at a time. Beat the egg whites until stiff but not dry, then fold into the spinach mixture.

Heavily butter a 15 x 11 x ½-inch jelly-roll pan, then line with waxed paper and butter the paper. Sprinkle evenly with the bread crumbs. Spread spinach mixture in prepared pan with a rubber spatula. Sprinkle with the grated Parmesan cheese. Bake in a preheated 350 degree oven for 15 to 18 minutes or until center feels firm but resilient when lightly touched with a fingertip. Remove from the oven and cover top with buttered waxed paper or foil. Invert onto a warm platter and remove paper lining adhered to roll. Spread roll with Shrimp Paste (recipe follows) and roll up gently with the aid of the paper or foil. Serve warm with Shrimp Sauce (recipe follows).

Shrimp Paste

2½ **pounds raw, shelled, deveined shrimp**
 1 **garlic clove**
 1 **bay leaf**
 ⅓ **cup wine vinegar**
 1 **cup softened butter, cut in pieces**
 ¾ **teaspoon onion juice**
 ½ **teaspoon mace**

Cook shrimp in boiling salted water with garlic, bay leaf and vinegar. Three minutes after it comes back to the boil should be ample. Remove shrimp and cool. Reserve ½ pound shrimp and 1½ cups shrimp liquor for Shrimp Sauce. With the metal blade in place, add ½ the shrimp, ½ the butter and ½ the seasonings to the beaker. Process until smooth. Transfer to a bowl and repeat the process with remaining shrimp, butter and seasonings. Combine mixtures and add salt, if necessary.

Shrimp Sauce

½ cup loosely packed
   parsley sprigs
1/8 cup loosely packed
   tarragon leaves *or*
1 teaspoon dried
   tarragon leaves,
   crumbled
½ pound cooked
   shrimp (reserved
   from Shrimp Paste)
4 tablespoons butter
3½ tablespoons flour
1½ cups shrimp liquor
   (reserved from
   Shrimp Paste)
1 teaspoon salt
½ teaspoon black pepper
1 teaspoon paprika
1/8 teaspoon mace

With the metal blade in place, add the parsley and
tarragon to beaker. Process until chopped. Remove
and add shrimp. Process, turning on and off
rapidly, until coarsely chopped. Melt butter in a
saucepan and blend in flour. Gradually stir in
boiling shrimp liquor and cook, stirring frequently,
until thickened, about 5 minutes. Season with salt,
pepper, paprika and mace. Add shrimp, parsley and
tarragon. Makes 8 servings, about 10 ounces each.

Salmon Pâté

1 to 1¼ pounds
   salmon fillets, skin
   removed and cut in
   1-inch strips
¼ cup Cognac
¼ cup Port wine
¼ teaspoon white
   pepper
2/3 cup water
1½ tablespoons butter
¼ teaspoon salt
2/3 cup flour
½ pound pike fillets or
   any non-oily white
   fish, cut in 1-inch
   pieces
6 tablespoons butter,
   cut in pieces
   Salt and pepper to
   taste
   Dash of nutmeg
1 egg
2 egg yolks
   Pork siding, sliced
¼ cup pistachio nuts
2 truffles, sliced or
   chopped (optional)

Combine salmon, Cognac, wine and white pepper.
Marinate for 30 minutes. Meanwhile, combine the
water, the 1½ tablespoons butter and ¼ teaspoon
salt in a saucepan. Bring to a boil, then add flour and
cook over low heat, stirring, until mixture forms a ball.
With the metal blade in place, add the panade to the
beaker. Process about 10 seconds. Add the pike,
the 6 tablespoons butter, salt, pepper and nutmeg.
Process, turning on and off occasionally, until well
mixed. Add egg and egg yolks. Process until smooth.
   Line a 6-cup terrine or loaf pan with pork slices.
Add a layer of pike mixture, pistachio nuts and
truffles. Drain salmon, reserving the marinade. Add
½ the salmon strips as next layer. Top with rest of
pike mixture, salmon and pork. Pour marinade over
all. Seal entire top with a paste of flour and water.
Add cover or cover with double layer of aluminum
foil tied tightly around top. Place in deep pan. Add
water 2/3 way up sides of terrine. Bring to boil, then
simmer for 2 hours. Remove paste and pork strips.
Chill thoroughly. Serve cold with Dijon Mayonnaise*.
Makes 1 loaf.

*Dijon Mayonnaise: To 1¾ cups Mayonnaise
(page 67), add 1 cup sour cream, 2 tablespoons
tomato paste, 2 chopped pimientos, 2 tablespoons
Cognac, 1 tablespoon Dijon mustard and
1 teaspoon Tabasco and process to mix thoroughly.

Adaptations

One service the Food Processor can do for you is to help you not only with new ideas, but with your long cherished and established recipes and menus. It's not impossible—in fact it is highly simple—to go through your repertoire and review your recipes and then figure out how the processor can act as another person in your kitchen.

Take a long recipe, for instance, that has a number of ingredients. Analyze those ingredients and see if there isn't some way that you can prepare quite a few of them without having to wash out the beaker of the processor, and, if you have two beakers for your unit, it makes it that much simpler. Say that you have a recipe that has several fresh herbs, nuts, and it might have onion. All these things can be processed and made ready for the recipe without having to take the beaker and wash it out each time and put it back and get ready. It's a simple process to adapt your life to the processor.

The same thing applies to menus. Plan menus where you can use your processor as often and as much as possible, and thus save yourself a good deal of added work. If you're entertaining or offering a meal that is complicated to several people, plan for the greatest help from the processor. This is one of the primary services of the machine, and one that I learned very early in my experience with it, and, one I have been able to adapt to my classes. It is simple to teach, or to cook, when many monotonous little processes can be done with a minimum of care and a maximum of processor.

Chinese Roast Pork

4 **pork tenderloins (each about ½ pound)** *or*

2 **pounds boned pork loin, trimmed of fat and cut in half**

¼ **cup soy sauce**

1 **tablespoon sugar**

1 **garlic clove, chopped**

¼ **cup whiskey**

1 **piece (about 1 inch) peeled fresh ginger, chopped**

Original Recipe

Place pork in shallow baking dish. Mix together the soy sauce, sugar, garlic, whiskey and ginger. Pour over pork, turning meat to coat all sides. Cover and let marinate in refrigerator several hours, turning occasionally. To cook, broil at low heat for 1 hour or, if desired, roast by weaving tenderloins on a spit. Serve hot or cold, cut in thin slices. A Chinese mustard made by mixing dry mustard with beer is sometimes served with this. Makes about 10 appetizer servings.

Food Processor Adaptation

This delicious appetizer is fast and easy to prepare when you let the Cuisinart Food Processor help you in these three ways:

to chop the garlic
to chop the ginger
to slice the pork

The garlic and ginger are used together and can be chopped together. Add them to the beaker of the processor, fitted with the metal blade, and process until finely chopped. Scrape the bowl clean and rinse it. If you wish to slice the cooked pork in the food processor, let it stand 20 to 30 minutes after cooking, then fit the slicing disk into the food processor. Cut a tenderloin in half and place both halves upright in the feed tube. Slice, using moderate pressure on the pusher.

Ducklings with Olive Sauce

2 **young ducklings**
Vegetable oil
Salt and pepper to taste

¼ **cup finely chopped onion**

¼ **cup butter**

1 **cup dry white wine**

1 **cup small pitted green Spanish olives**

Original Recipe

Use only young ducklings with as little fat as possible. Split ducklings in half. Rub bone side with a little vegetable oil and grill, bone side down, for 25 minutes. Season skin side with salt and pepper. Turn and grill, skin side down, for 15 or 20 minutes or until skin is browned and crispy. While ducklings cook, prepare sauce. Sauté onion in butter until soft. Add wine, olives and salt and pepper to taste. Cook over low heat for 5 minutes. Serve over ducklings. Makes 4 servings.

Adaptations

Food Processor Adaptation

The Cuisinart Food Processor will aid you in preparing these ducklings in two ways:

to chop the onion
to slice the olives

Chop the onion first, using the metal blade and cutting a small onion into halves before adding it to the beaker of the processor. Then, empty the beaker and, with the slicing disk in place, slice the olives. There is no need to wash the beaker between operations.

Beefsteak Bismarck

2 **pounds ground beef**
2 **tablespoons melted butter**
¼ **cup finely chopped green onions**
1 **teaspoon salt**
½ **teaspoon black pepper**
2 **beefsteak tomatoes, halved**
  Fine bread crumbs
  Salt and pepper to taste
  Melted butter
4 **eggs**
  Bacon fat or butter
  Chopped parsley or basil

Original Recipe

Mix together beef, the 2 tablespoons butter, onions, salt and pepper. Form into 4 patties and grill until done to your taste. Sprinkle tomato halves with bread crumbs and salt and pepper. Brush with melted butter. Arrange in baking dish and broil until heated through, but not overcooked or mushy. Meanwhile, fry eggs in bacon fat or butter. To serve, arrange hamburgers on plates and top each with a fried egg. Garnish with a broiled tomato half, sprinkled with chopped parsley or finely cut fresh basil, if available. Makes 4 servings.

Food Processor Adaptation

The Cuisinart Food Processor will help you in four ways with this recipe:

to grind the beef
to chop the onions
to prepare the bread crumbs
to chop the parsley

Using the metal blade, chop the parsley first since the beaker should be clean for this. Then, remove the parsley and, using the metal blade again, process a slice of bread which has been torn into chunks or quarters. If a few bits of parsley are left in the beaker, it doesn't matter. Empty the beaker again. Cut the onions and beef into 1-inch pieces. Chop them together, using ½ pound beef (1 well-packed measuring cup) and ¼ the onions at a time. Use the metal blade and process by turning on and off rapidly for an even chop. The meat is ground last because it leaves a film of fat and the beaker must then be washed.

Crown Roast of Pork with Chestnut Stuffing

1 cup finely chopped
   onions
½ cup melted butter
2 garlic cloves, finely
   chopped
2 teaspoons salt
¼ teaspoon freshly
   ground black pepper
1 teaspoon dried sage
   leaves
2 cups soft bread
   crumbs
1 cup canned whole
   chestnuts, drained
½ cup Madeira or sherry
¼ cup chopped
   parsley
1 pork crown roast,
   about 7 pounds
   Salt, pepper, nutmeg
3 tablespoons flour
1½ cups heavy cream

Original Recipe

Sauté onions in melted butter until just limp. Add garlic, salt, pepper and sage. Combine mixture with bread crumbs, chestnuts, wine, parsley and additional butter, if needed. Rub pork with salt, pepper and nutmeg. Wrap bone ends with foil. Fill center with stuffing and dot with additional butter. Place roast on foil-covered rack in baking pan. Roast in preheated 325 degree oven, allowing 20 minutes per pound and basting from time to time with additional butter and wine heated together.

When roast is done, place on platter and keep warm. Heat 3 tablespoons pan drippings with flour, stirring until smooth. Gradually stir in cream and cook, stirring until smooth and thickened. Add salt and pepper to taste. Serve pork with this cream sauce and, if desired, 2 cups applesauce combined with 3 to 4 tablespoons grated horseradish. Makes about 12 servings, 1 rib each.

Food Processor Adaptation

Use the Cuisinart Food Processor in four ways to ease the preparation of this stuffed crown roast:

to chop the onions
to chop the garlic
to prepare the bread crumbs
to chop the parsley

Chopping the onions and garlic will leave the beaker wet with onion juice, so chop the bread crumbs and the parsley first as they will be used together. Use the metal blade and add 4 slices of bread, each torn into quarters, and 1 cup loosely packed parsley to the beaker. After processing, scrape the mixture into a bowl and reserve. Put the butter in a skillet over low heat. While it is melting, chop the onion and garlic together in the beaker using the metal blade. Scrape the mixture into the melted butter and proceed with the recipe. If you want finely chopped garlic and coarsely chopped onion, chop the garlic finely, then cut the onion in quarters, add it to the beaker and turn the machine on and off 4 or 5 times.

Rolled Stuffed Fillets of Sole

4 **slices bacon, finely
chopped**
2 **medium onions,
finely chopped**
1 **garlic clove, chopped**
¼ **pound mushrooms,
finely chopped**
1 **small dill pickle,
finely chopped**
1 **small tomato, peeled,
seeded and chopped
Salt and freshly
ground black pepper**
8 **large fillets of sole,
about 6 ounces each**
½ **cup dry white wine**
8 **thin lemon slices**

Original Recipe

Cook the bacon in a heavy skillet discarding some
of the fat during cooking and leaving about
2 tablespoons. Add the onions, garlic and
mushrooms. Sauté gently until soft and well
blended. Add the pickle, tomato and seasonings.
Cook 2 or 3 minutes more. Spread fish fillets with
stuffing mixture and roll up, starting at the wide
end. Fasten with toothpicks, if necessary, and
arrange in a shallow buttered baking dish. Pour in
the wine and bake in preheated 350 degree oven for
20 minutes or until done but not dry. Garnish each
serving with a lemon slice and, if you like, a few
small cooked shrimps. Makes 8 servings.

Food Processor Adaptation

In preparing these stuffed fillets, the Cuisinart
Food Processor can simplify the task in seven
different ways:

to chop the bacon
to chop the garlic
to chop the onions
to chop the mushrooms
to chop the pickles
to chop the tomatoes
to slice the lemon

Bacon is the first ingredient listed that requires
chopping. Cut the bacon into pieces and use the
metal blade to process it until finely chopped.
Remove the bacon to a skillet. While it cooks, use
the metal blade again to chop the garlic. Without
removing the garlic, add the onions, cut into
quarters, and the mushrooms. (These can be
chopped together because they are cooked
together.) Chop coarsely and remove from the
beaker. Next, add the dill pickle, cut into 1-inch
pieces, and the peeled, seeded and quartered
tomato and process to chop them. When ready for
the garnish, use the slicing disk, to slice the lemon.
Cut off one end of the lemon and insert it, cut side
down into the feed tube. Slice, using firm pressure
on pusher.

Turkey with Tarragon Stuffing

1 **turkey (12-14 pounds)**
Salt
Lemon
2 **cups water**
2 **teaspoons salt**
1 **cup finely chopped**
shallots
6 **tablespoons butter**
2 **to 3 teaspoons dried**
tarragon leaves
2 **teaspoons salt**
8 **cups soft bread**
crumbs
1 **cup pine nuts or**
coarsely chopped
toasted almonds
¾ **cup butter, melted**
½ **cup chopped parsley**
3 **tablespoons flour**
Salt and pepper
2 **tablespoons Cognac**
16 **to 18 thin pork**
sausages, cooked
Watercress or
parsley sprigs

Original Recipe

Rub the inside of the turkey with salt and lemon. Put neck and giblets in saucepan with water and the 2 teaspoons salt. Bring to a boil, then reduce heat and simmer, covered, for 1 hour. Reserve giblets and strain broth. Sauté shallots in 6 tablespoons butter in a heavy skillet until soft. Add tarragon, 2 teaspoons salt, bread crumbs, nuts, melted butter and parsley. Toss well and taste for seasoning.

Stuff and truss turkey, closing the vent with several thicknesses of foil. Place on one side on rack in roasting pan. Butter well and drape with foil. Roast in preheated 350 degree oven for 1 hour. Turn on other side and roast for another hour. Turn on back, remove foil and roast until leg moves easily, basting from time to time. Sprinkle bird well with salt and pepper and let rest for 15 minutes on a hot platter before carving. Combine 4 tablespoons pan drippings with the flour in a heavy skillet over medium heat. Stir in the reserved broth. Cook until thickened. Season to taste with salt and pepper. Add Cognac, chopped liver and heart. Garnish platter with sausages and sprigs of watercress or parsley.

Food Processor Adaptation

The Cuisinart Food Processor can assist you five ways with this recipe:

to chop the shallots
to prepare the bread crumbs
to chop the almonds
to chop the parsley
to chop the liver and heart

Use the metal blade for all procedures and empty the beaker after each. Chop the shallots first. While they are sautéing, prepare the bread crumbs. Eight cups of crumbs are needed. Make 2 cups at a time, using 4 slices of bread, each torn into quarters, and several sprigs of parsley. (Always chop bread and parsley together if the recipe calls for them to be used together.)

If almonds are used instead of pine nuts, process them only until coarsely chopped. Chop the liver and heart last, turning the processor on and off rapidly, because they will give off the most liquid. This way you can go through all five procedures without washing the beaker until all the chopping is completed.

Lahma Bi Ajeen

(Arab version of pizza)

Dough:

1 **package active dry yeast**
  Pinch of sugar
1 **to 1½ cups warm water (110 to 115 degrees)**
3¾ **cups unbleached all-purpose flour**
1 **teaspoon salt**
2 **tablespoons olive oil**

Filling:

3 **large onions, chopped**
2 **garlic cloves, chopped**
1 **tablespoon olive oil**
1½ **pounds boneless lamb shoulder, finely ground**
½ **cup pine nuts**
3 **tablespoons tomato paste**
1 **teaspoon sugar**
¾ **teaspoon ground allspice**
1 **tablespoon lemon juice**
1 **tablespoon plus 1 teaspoon salt**
1 **teaspoon cracked black pepper**
2 **drops Tabasco**
3 **tablespoons chopped parsley**

Original Recipe

To prepare dough, dissolve yeast with sugar in ½ cup warm water and let stand in warm place until foamy, about 10 minutes. Put flour and salt in a large warm mixing bowl. Make a well in the center and add oil and yeast mixture. Work dough vigorously, adding remaining warm water to make a soft dough. Knead until pliable and elastic, about 15 minutes. Place in greased bowl, turning to coat all sides. Cover with damp cloth and set in warm place until doubled in bulk, about 2 or 3 hours.

Meanwhile, prepare filling. Sauté onions and garlic in olive oil until onions are wilted but not brown. Add to ground meat along with rest of ingredients and mix well.

Turn out dough on lightly floured board and knead a few times. Divide into 8 pieces, shape each into a ball and let rest for a few minutes. Roll each with a floured rolling pin into a circle 5 to 6 inches in diameter. Press around edge of each to form a rim, then spread prepared filling generously on each. Transfer to lightly oiled baking sheet and bake in preheated 450 to 500 degree oven for 8 to 10 minutes. Makes 8 servings.

Food Processor Adaptation

The Cuisinart Food Processor can help you prepare this hors d'oeuvre, which is great for cocktail parties, in four ways:

to prepare the dough
to chop the onions
to mince the garlic
to grind the lamb

The recipe calls for 3¾ cups flour which is ¾ cup too much for the capacity of the beaker. Since the processor works so fast, the dough can easily be mixed in two batches. Proof the yeast in ½ cup warm water with a pinch of sugar. With the metal blade in place, add 2 cups flour, ½ teaspoon salt, 1 tablespoon oil and ½ the proofed yeast. Have ready ½ cup warm water. While processing, pour in ¼ cup water, then dribble in the remaining water only until a ball of dough forms on the metal blades (all the water may not be necessary). Repeat with the second batch using remaining flour. Knead both doughs together, place in greased bowl and allow to rise as in the original recipe.

For the filling, chop the garlic, using the metal blade. Without removing the garlic, add the onions, quartered, and process turning on and off until finely chopped. While the onions and garlic are sautéing, grind the lamb in ½ pound batches. Cut the lamb into cubes before adding it to the beaker and process by turning on and off rapidly for an even chop.

Weeping Leg of Lamb

1 small (4½ to 5 pounds) leg of lamb
3 garlic cloves, cut in slivers
Salt and pepper to taste
1 teaspoon dried rosemary leaves
6 to 8 potatoes, peeled, thinly sliced and washed
¼ cup butter
1 small onion, thinly sliced
1 cup beef bouillon

Original Recipe

Trim leg of lamb well and insert garlic slivers. Rub with salt, pepper and rosemary. Dry potatoes thoroughly and arrange in layers in a buttered baking dish that is as long as the leg of lamb. Add salt and pepper and dots of butter after each layer and add onion slices after second layer. Add bouillon. Place lamb on potatoes or on an oven rack over the potatoes.

Roast in preheated 325 degree oven until lamb is rare, 135 degrees internal temperature, and potatoes are nicely browned and crusty. This will take about 1¾ to 2 hours. If potatoes are done first, remove them and continue cooking the lamb. Return potatoes to oven for 10 minutes to reheat before serving. If desired, sprinkle with grated Parmesan cheese. Makes 8 servings.

Adaptations

Food Processor Adaptation

In preparing this Weeping Leg of Lamb, the Cuisinart Food Processor will help you in these four ways:

to slice the potatoes
to slice the onion
to slice the butter
to grate the Parmesan cheese

First, chop the Parmesan cheese, using the metal blade. Cut the cheese into pieces. Start the processor and drop the pieces through the feed tube, a few at a time. Process until it is as fine as you desire. Remove the cheese. Since potatoes discolor quickly when exposed to air, slice the onion first, using the slicing disk. Remove the onion slices and, with the slicing disk in place again, slice the potatoes which have been cut into lengthwise halves or quarters so they can easily slide through the feed tube. Lastly, slice ½ stick of cold butter for dotting the vegetables. If more is needed, slice more.

Seafood Sausages

¾ **pound sole or pike fillets**
1 **egg white***
⅔ **cup heavy cream**
½ **teaspoon salt**
1/8 **teaspoon pepper**
 Dash of paprika
3 **drops Tabasco**
¼ **cup parsley, finely chopped**
¼ **cup mushrooms, finely chopped**
¼ **cup scallops, finely chopped**
2 **tablespoons salmon, finely chopped**
 Meat of a 1¼ to 1½ pound lobster, finely chopped *or* **⅓ cup shrimp or crabmeat, finely chopped**
2 **to 3 feet sausage casing**
 Vegetable oil

Original Recipe

Purée fish fillets, using a meat grinder. Transfer to a large bowl and place over ice water. Beat in egg white and mix well. Gradually stir in cream, a teaspoon at a time, then season with salt, pepper, paprika and Tabasco. Taste and adjust seasoning. Stir in parsley, mushrooms, scallops, salmon and lobster meat.

Using a sausage stuffer or funnel, stuff mixture into casings which have been rinsed in water. Try to eliminate air bubbles. Prick with a fork. Poach gently in salted water for 1½ hours. Drain and brown quickly in oil. Serve with a Velouté or Nantua Sauce. Makes 8 to 10 servings.

*When using a food processor, substitute 1 whole egg.

Food Processor Adaptation

The Cuisinart Food Processor can save you an hour's time on this recipe for Seafood Sausages by helping you in six ways:

to chop the parsley
to chop the mushrooms
to chop the salmon
to chop the lobster
to chop the scallops
to prepare the mousse

Using the metal blade for all procedures, chop the parsley and mushrooms first because they will leave the bowl clean. They are used together and can be chopped together. Next, chop the salmon and lobster together, then chop the scallops separately. The scallops are chopped last because they give off the most liquid and make it necessary to rinse the beaker. Make the mousse by processing the pike, cut in pieces, and the egg until a smooth paste is formed. Gradually pour in the cream while processing, then add the seasonings. Without a food processor, it would take about 45 minutes to prepare this mousse. The fish fillets would have to be placed over a bowl of ice to enable an egg white to be beaten into the mixture. A whole egg could not be used. It would not emulsify. The cream would have to be added a teaspoon at a time.

Veal Chops, Ann de Beaujeu

3 medium onions, chopped
6 tablespoons butter
3 tablespoons flour
⅔ cup heavy cream
2½ ounces Gruyère or Switzerland Swiss cheese, shredded (⅔ cup)
Dash of nutmeg
Salt and pepper to taste
4 veal chops
Flour
1 egg, beaten
Butter

Original Recipe

Combine onions and butter in heavy skillet or saucepan. Cover and allow to steam over low heat until onions are soft and a good deal of liquid has been drawn out. Force onion mixture through a fine sieve, reserving 3 tablespoons butter-onion liquid in skillet. Blend in flour and cook until well thickened. Add sieved onion mixture and stir over low heat until blended and thickened. Add cream and ½ cup of the cheese. Cook, stirring, until cheese is melted. Add nutmeg, salt and pepper. Dip veal chops into flour, beaten egg and again into flour. Sauté in butter until well browned on both sides. Arrange in shallow baking dish. Spoon sauce over veal chops and sprinkle with remaining cheese. Place in a very hot oven or under the broiler long enough to melt the cheese. Makes 4 servings.

Food Processor Adaptation

These veal chops are simple and easy to prepare when you let the Cuisinart Food Processor help you in these four ways:

to shred the cheese
to chop the raw onion
to "sieve" the cooked onion
to combine cooked onion, cheese and cream

First, shred the cheese since it will leave the beaker of the processor clean. Use the shredding disk and cut the cheese into pieces that will fit the feed tube. Remove the shredding disk and reserve the cheese. With the metal blade in place, add the onions, cut into quarters, and process by turning on and off rapidly until the onions are finely chopped. Cook, covered, in butter, as indicated in the original recipe. When onions are soft, return them to the beaker. Blend flour into butter-onion liquid.

While flour is cooking, process onions 15 seconds or until nearly smooth. Add ½ cup shredded cheese and process again, adding the ⅔ cup heavy cream, until well mixed. Gradually add beaker contents to onion-flour mixture, stirring until thickened. Add seasonings. Continue with original recipe.

Rack of Lamb, Quo Vadis

1 **rack of lamb, about 6 chops**
 Butter
 Pepper
2 **small carrots, minced**
1 **medium onion, minced**
1 **tablespoon butter**
1 **cup stock (lamb or chicken)**
¼ **cup soft bread crumbs**
¼ **cup minced parsley**
 Watercress

Original Recipe

Trim excess fat from lamb. Wrap ends of rib bones with foil. Rub meat with butter and sprinkle with pepper. Spread minced carrots and onion in bottom of a shallow roasting pan. Dot with butter. Place lamb, fat side down, on vegetables. Roast in preheated 500 degree oven for 20 minutes. Reduce heat to 400 degrees. Turn lamb over and add ½ cup stock. Roast for 15 to 20 minutes. Sprinkle lamb with mixture of crumbs and parsley and slide under broiler for 4 or 5 minutes. Transfer to a hot platter. Add remaining ½ cup stock to pan, then purée the vegetable-stock mixture and correct for seasoning. Serve as a sauce with lamb. To serve, carve into chops or parallel to the bone in medium slices. Garnish platter with watercress. Makes 2 to 3 servings.

Food Processor Adaptation

This famous dish from one of New York's finest restaurants, Quo Vadis, is simple and easy when you let the Cuisinart Food Processor help you in five ways:

to prepare the bread crumbs
to mince the parsley
to mince the carrots
to mince the onion
to purée the sauce

The bread crumbs and parsley are used together in the recipe and they should be chopped together. With the metal blade in place, combine 1 bread slice, torn into quarters, and 8 to 10 sprigs of parsley in the beaker of the processor. Process until evenly chopped. Empty the beaker and reserve the crumbs and parsley mixture, covered. With the metal blade in place again, combine the onion, cut into quarters, and the carrots, cut into pieces. Process, turning on and off rapidly a few times, or until coarsley minced. Just before carving the chops, add the stock and vegetables to the beaker of the processor which again has been fitted with the metal blade. Process, turning on and off for about 6 seconds, then let run continuously for another 10 seconds to form a smooth purée.

Lasagna

3 garlic cloves, finely chopped
1 medium onion, chopped
6 tablespoons olive oil
1 29-oz. can Italian plum tomatoes
1 6-oz. can tomato paste
1 cup red wine or beer
1 teaspoon dried basil leaves
1 teaspoon salt
1 teaspoon pepper
¾ pound lasagna noodles
½ pound ground beef
½ pound ground pork
3 tablespoons butter
16 ounces ricotta cheese
1 pound mozzarella cheese, thinly sliced
Grated Parmesan cheese

Original Recipe

Sauté garlic and onion in olive oil until soft. Add tomatoes, tomato paste, red wine or beer, basil, salt and pepper. Simmer for 45 minutes. Strain sauce and keep warm. Cook noodles in boiling salted water until just tender. Drain. Put on paper towels to absorb moisture and prevent sticking. Brown meat quickly in butter. Arrange a layer of noodles in an oiled, straight-sided baking dish. Add layers of meat, sauce, ricotta cheese, mozzarella cheese and noodles, ending with noodles. Use only ½ the sauce. Sprinkle liberally with Parmesan cheese. Bake in preheated 350 degree oven for 20 minutes. Serve cut in squares with remaining sauce. Makes 6 servings.

Food Processor Adaptation

In preparing this Lasagna, the Cuisinart Food Processor can be used in five ways:

to grate the Parmesan cheese
to slice the mozzarella cheese
to chop the garlic
to chop the onion
to grind the meats together

First, grate the Parmesan cheese, using the metal blade. Cut the cheese into pieces. Start the processor and drop the pieces through the feed tube, a few at a time. Remove the cheese. Next, using the slicing disk, slice the mozzarella cheese which has been cut into pieces to fit the feed tube. Remove the cheese. Using the metal blade again, chop the garlic and onions. These can be chopped together because they are used together. If you prefer finely chopped garlic and coarsely chopped onions, chop the garlic first, then add the onions without removing the garlic. Scrape the mixture into a pan with olive oil and, while it is sautéing, grind the beef and pork together in ½ pound batches, turning the processor on and off rapidly. The meat is ground last because it will leave a slight film of fat on the beaker.

Quick Gratin Savoyard

4 medium (1¼ pounds) potatoes, peeled and sliced
1 pound chorizo or other sausage, sliced
Salt and pepper to taste
Flour
Butter
2 cups heavy cream
Grated Swiss or Parmesan cheese

Original Recipe

Place a layer of potato slices in a buttered 2-quart casserole. Add a layer of sausage slices, then sprinkle with salt, pepper and flour. Dot with butter. Repeat layers, ending with top layer of potatoes. Add cream and sprinkle top with cheese. Bake in preheated 375 degree oven for 30 minutes or until potatoes are tender. Uncover for last 10 minutes and add a little more cheese so top gets crusty. Makes 4 servings.

Food Processor Adaptation

The Cuisinart Food Processor will aid you in four ways:

to slice the potatoes
to slice the sausage
to grate the cheese
to slice the butter

It is necessary for the beaker to be clean when the cheese is grated. Do this first. Cut the cheese into cubes and use the metal blade. Start the processor and add the cheese through the feed tube, a few pieces at a time. Remove the cheese, scrape the beaker with a spatula and, using the slicing disk, slice the sausage. Remove the sausage slices and, again using the slicing disk, slice the potatoes which have been cut into lengthwise halves or quarters so they go through the feed tube easily. With the slicing disk in place, put chilled butter into feed tube and slice, using medium pressure.

Lamb Marrakech

3 pounds lean boneless lamb, leg or shoulder, cut in 1½-inch pieces
½ cup peanut or olive oil
2 large onions, chopped fine
3 garlic cloves, chopped
2 teaspoons salt
1 very small fresh hot red chili pepper or
½ teaspoon crushed dried red chili pepper
½ teaspoon Spice Parisienne*
1 teaspoon turmeric
3 large tomatoes, peeled, seeded and chopped
1 cup raisins, soaked in sherry
½ cup toasted almonds
½ cup toasted filberts
   Crisp fried onion rings
   Chopped parsley

Original Recipe

Brown the lamb in the oil. Add the onions and garlic and brown lightly. Add seasonings, tomatoes and raisins. Bring to boil, adding a small amount of liquid if necessary. Cover and simmer until tender, about 1½ hours, or place in preheated 350 degree oven and allow the same time, basting occasionally. If cooked in the oven, it may be necessary to cover the pan for half the time or add more liquid. Add almonds, filberts, onion rings and parsley; heat through. Serve with rice cooked with pine nuts. Makes 6 to 8 servings.

*For Spice Parisienne, put in beaker 1 teaspoon ground cinnamon, 2 teaspoons ground allspice, 1/8 teaspoon ground cloves, 1 teaspoon ground nutmeg, 2 teaspoons ground coriander, 2 teaspoons dried tarragon leaves and ½ teaspoon dried marjoram leaves. Process for 30 seconds. Keep in tightly closed container in dark place.

Food Processor Adaptation

This exciting lamb entrée is made seven ways
easier for you by the Cuisinart Food Processor:

to make the Spice Parisienne
to chop the parsley
to slice the onions for fried onion rings
to chop the onions
to chop the garlic
to chop the chili pepper
to chop the tomatoes

Since the Spice Parisienne will leave the bowl dry,
we should do this first. Add all the ingredients to
the beaker and combine, using the metal blade.
Remove and set aside. Add ½ cup loosely packed
parsley to the beaker and chop, using the metal
blade. Remove and set aside for garnish. Cut one
medium onion into pieces that will fit easily into
feed tube. With the slicing disk in place, slice the
onion, using medium pressure. Fry sliced onions
until crisp and set aside for garnish.

The garlic, onions and pepper are cooked
together and they can be processed together. First,
using the metal blade, chop the garlic. Then,
without removing the garlic, add the onions cut into
quarters, and the hot chili pepper. Process, turning
on and off, until the ingredients are finely chopped.
Next, without washing the beaker and with the
metal blade in place, add the tomatoes which have
been peeled, seeded and quartered. Process,
turning on and off, just a few times until evenly
chopped.

Vegetables

Purée of Peas

3 pounds fresh peas,
shelled *or*
3 10-oz. packages
frozen peas
1 small carrot, cut in
pieces
2 scallions, cut in
halves
½ cup water
Salt and pepper to
taste
¼ teaspoon dried thyme
leaves
4 tablespoons butter,
cut in pieces
½ cup heavy cream

Place peas, carrot, scallions, water and seasonings
in a saucepan. Bring to a boil, then reduce heat and
simmer, covered, until peas are tender. Drain and
discard carrot and scallions. With the metal blade
in place, add peas to the beaker. Process until
smooth. Add butter and heavy cream. Process
again until combined. Taste purée for salt and
pepper. Transfer to a baking dish and set in pan of
hot water. Bake in preheated 300 degree oven until
heated through, about 20 minutes. Dot top with
additional butter before serving. Makes 8 servings.

Cabbage Custard

1 **small head cabbage, about 2 pounds, cored and cut in wedges to fit feed tube**
3 **slices white bread, cut in pieces**
½ **pound sharp Cheddar cheese**
2 **eggs**
1 **teaspoon salt**
2 **tablespoons Dijon mustard**
2 **cups milk**

With the slicing disk in place, slice cabbage, feeding wedges through the feed tube with the pusher. Place sliced cabbage (there should be 4 cups) in a large kettle and cover with cold water. Bring to boil, then reduce heat and simmer, covered, until just tender. Drain immediately. Place ½ the cabbage in a buttered 2-quart baking dish.

With the metal blade in place, add the bread to the beaker. Process, turning on and off rapidly, to make fine crumbs. Remove the metal blade and insert the shredding disk. Shred cheese over the bread crumbs. Remove shredding disk. Mix crumbs and cheese together. Sprinkle ½ the mixture over cabbage in baking dish. Add another layer of cabbage, then top with rest of cheese and bread crumbs.

With the metal blade in place, add the eggs, salt and Dijon mustard to the beaker. Process until blended. Pour milk through the feed tube and process for another 5 seconds to combine completely. Immediately pour egg and milk mixture over cabbage. Press down lightly with hands. Allow to rest for 20 minutes, then bake in preheated 350 degree oven for 30 minutes. Makes 6 to 8 serving

Potato Shreds

These are excellent served in place of French fries or as an accompaniment for such dishes as broiled chicken or roast rack of lamb.

6 **medium (2 pounds) potatoes, peeled and quartered**
Peanut oil for frying

With the shredding disk in place, fill the feed tube of food processor with potato quarters, placing them cut side down. Shred, using firm pressure on the pusher. Transfer potato shreds to a bowl containing cold water. Potatoes may be held at this point for several hours before frying. Just before ready to serve, drain potatoes and pat dry. It is essential that the potatoes be very dry.

Fry about 1/8 the potato shreds at a time in deep oil at 375 degrees until golden brown, about 5 to 8 minutes. It is necessary to fry the potato shreds in 4 or more batches so that the potatoes will not lower the temperature of the oil too much. Makes 4 to 5 cups.

Simone Beck's Zucchini Bramafam

If you like zucchini, this is a dish made quick and easy by the food processor. With a good steak or any broiled meat, this attractive vegetable dish is delicious.

1½ **pounds small zucchini squash**
2 **tablespoons salt**
¼ **cup butter**
2 **tablespoons olive oil**
Freshly ground black pepper
Freshly grated nutmeg
2 **or 3 tablespoons Crème Fraîche (page 67) or sour cream**
2 **tablespoons minced fresh herbs (parsley, chervil, basil)**

Cut zucchini in half lengthwise. With the slicing disk in place, stand the zucchini upright in feed tube of food processor. Slice, using moderate pressure on the pusher. Transfer slices to a large mixing bowl and sprinkle with salt. Let stand 20 minutes, then drain thoroughly. To remove additional water, squeeze zucchini, a handful at a time, in corner of a kitchen towel.

Heat butter and oil in a saucepan. Add zucchini and stir until soft, about 3 to 5 minutes. Season highly with pepper and nutmeg. Add Crème Fraîche or sour cream and serve sprinkled with fresh herbs. Makes 4 servings.

Duxelles

Duxelles is a preparation of mushrooms finely chopped and sautéed in lots of butter. It can be an exciting flavoring for soups and sauces, a beautiful streak through scrambled eggs for breakfast and one of the most versatile flavorings we have in our cooking repertoire.

2 **pounds mushrooms, cut in pieces**
1 **cup butter**
Salt and pepper to taste

With the metal blade in place, add 6 to 8 mushrooms at a time to the beaker of food processor, making sure that the beaker is never more than half filled. Process, turning on and off rapidly, until mushrooms are finely chopped, about 8 to 10 seconds. Transfer to a large bowl and repeat until all the mushrooms are chopped. Place mushrooms in a kitchen towel and squeeze out all liquid. (You can save the liquid for flavoring sauces or for use in vegetable stock.)

Melt the butter in a large heavy skillet. Add the mushrooms and cook very slowly, stirring occasionally, until all liquid disappears and the mushrooms form a dark, dense mass. Taste and add salt and pepper. Mix well. Duxelles freezes well. Makes about 2½ cups.

Julie Dannenbaum's Acorn Squash

1 **medium acorn squash**
¼ **slice bread**
2 **shallots, halved**
¼ **cup loosely packed parsley sprigs**
2 **tablespoons butter**
2 **tablespoons sour cream**
  Salt and pepper to taste
2 **teaspoons melted butter**

Cut squash lengthwise into halves. Remove seeds and fibrous material with the tip of a tablespoon. Place halves cut side down on rack of shallow baking pan. Pour hot water into pan ½ way up sides of pan. Place in preheated 350 degree oven for 35 to 40 minutes to allow squash to steam and soften. When soft, remove from oven and allow to cool slightly.

With the metal blade in place, add bread and process until you have fine crumbs. Remove and set aside. Add the shallots and parsley to the beaker. Process until evenly chopped. Add scooped out squash, reserving shells, butter, sour cream, salt and pepper. Process until smooth. Taste and adjust seasoning. Spoon mixture into squash shells. Sprinkle each with mixture of bread crumbs and melted butter. Bake in preheated 350 degree oven for 15 to 20 minutes. If prepared ahead and refrigerated, allow 25 to 30 minutes baking time. Makes 2 servings.

John Clancy's Broccoli Mold

1 **bunch broccoli, about 1½ pounds**
3 **eggs**
¼ **cup heavy cream**
1½ **teaspoons salt**
¼ **teaspoon freshly ground black pepper**
1/8 **teaspoon freshly ground nutmeg**

Drain broccoli in colander after cooking it in salted water until tender. Let cool to room temperature, then cut in pieces. With the metal blade in place, add ⅓ broccoli pieces to the beaker. Process until finely chopped. Repeat 2 times, adding ½ remaining broccoli each time to chopped broccoli in beaker. If necessary, stop processing and scrape down sides with spatula. Add eggs, one at a time, processing after each addition until mixed in. Add cream, salt, pepper and nutmeg. Process until smooth. Spoon mixture into a buttered 3 to 4-cup ring mold. Cover with buttered wax paper, placing buttered side down. Place mold in shallow roasting pan on oven shelf. Pour boiling water into pan to depth ½ way up sides of mold. Bake in preheated 350 degree oven 30 minutes or until knife inserted in center of custard comes out clean. To unmold, invert round serving plate on mold, then turn over and lift off mold. Makes 5 to 6 servings.

Cauliflower Purée

1 **medium head cauliflower**
2 **teaspoons lemon juice**
6 **tablespoons sweet butter, cut in pieces**
1 **teaspoon salt**
1/8 **teaspoon freshly ground black pepper**

Drain cauliflower in colander after cooking it in salted water until tender. Let cool to room temperature, then cut in pieces. With the metal blade in place, add ⅓ cauliflower pieces and the lemon juice to the beaker. Process until finely chopped, about 3 to 4 seconds. Repeat 2 times, adding ½ remaining cauliflower pieces each time to chopped cauliflower in the beaker. If necessary, stop processing and scrape down sides with spatula. Add butter, salt and pepper. Process until smooth, about 10 seconds. Makes 4 to 6 servings.

Variation: For a cauliflower loaf or soufflé, insert shredding disk and shred ¼ pound Cheddar cheese, cut in strips to fit feed tube. Remove shredding disk and insert metal blade. Proceed with Cauliflower Purée recipe, adding ingredients to cheese in beaker. Add 2 tablespoons Dijon mustard with other seasonings. Remove to a large bowl. Fold in 4 egg whites, beaten stiff but not dry. Pour into a buttered 4-cup loaf pan or soufflé dish. Place in a shallow baking pan and fill pan with boiling water to depth ½ way up sides of loaf pan or soufflé dish. Bake in preheated 350 degree oven for 1 hour.

Carrot Purée

10 **to 12 carrots, about 1½ pounds, cut in pieces**
¼ **cup butter, cut in pieces**
1 **teaspoon salt**
¼ **teaspoon pepper**
2 **tablespoons heavy cream**
1 **tablespoon Cognac**

Cook carrots in boiling, salted water until tender; drain. With the metal blade in place, add ⅓ the carrot pieces to the beaker. Process until finely chopped. Repeat 2 times, adding ½ remaining carrots each time to chopped carrots in bowl. If necessary, stop processing and scrape down sides with spatula. Add butter, salt and pepper. Process until smooth, about 30 seconds. Add cream and Cognac. Process again until combined. Taste for salt and pepper and perhaps additional Cognac or butter. To make an absolutely smooth purée, process for an additional 30 seconds, then press through a fine sieve. Makes about 4 servings.

Variation: For a carrot loaf or soufflé, leave puréed carrots in beaker of food processor and add 3 egg yolks and 1 slice white bread, cut in pieces. Process, turning on and off, until smooth. Fold in 4 egg whites, beaten stiff but not dry. Pour into buttered 1-quart loaf pan or soufflé dish. Place in shallow baking pan and fill pan with boiling water to depth ½ way up sides of loaf pan or soufflé dish. Bake in preheated 350 degree oven for 1 hour.

Yams

2 **pounds yams, peeled and cut in quarters**	Cook yams until tender in boiling salted water. Drain. With the metal blade in place, add ½ the
½ **teaspoon nutmeg**	yams to the beaker. Process, turning on and off
¾ **teaspoon salt**	rapidly, until evenly chopped, about 20 seconds.
Dash of cloves	Leave in beaker. Add remaining yams, nutmeg,

2 **pounds yams, peeled and cut in quarters**
½ **teaspoon nutmeg**
¾ **teaspoon salt**
Dash of cloves
2 **tablespoons sugar**
2 **tablespoons butter**
1 **egg**
¼ **cup heavy cream**
1 **2-inch square orange peel**
1 **2-inch square lemon peel**

Cook yams until tender in boiling salted water. Drain. With the metal blade in place, add ½ the yams to the beaker. Process, turning on and off rapidly, until evenly chopped, about 20 seconds. Leave in beaker. Add remaining yams, nutmeg, salt, cloves, sugar, butter, egg, cream, orange peel and lemon peel. Process, turning on and off for 20 seconds, then let run until smooth. Pour into buttered 1-quart soufflé dish. If desired, sprinkle top lightly with brown sugar and dot with additional butter. Bake in preheated 350 degree oven for 35 minutes. Makes 6 to 8 servings.

Simca's Crème de Champignons Campanette

This mushroom dish is a beautiful accompaniment for fish, or it can be used as a garnish for any white meat or a stuffing for fish or poultry. It's also delicious with eggs.

1 **pound mushrooms**
Juice of 1 lemon
¼ **cup peeled shallots (substitute scallions if not available)**
3 **tablespoons butter**
1 **cup light cream**
Salt
Freshly ground white pepper
2 **tablespoons Crème Fraîche (page 67) or sour cream**

Separate the stems from the caps of the mushrooms; reserve stems for another use. With the slicing disk in place, cover the beaker and stack mushrooms in feed tube of food processor, standing them on edge. Slice, using moderate pressure on the pusher. Remove to a bowl and sprinkle with lemon juice. With the metal blade in place, add the shallots to the beaker. Process until finely chopped.

Melt butter in a skillet. Add shallots and sauté until they are just beginning to become tender, about 2 or 3 minutes. Add mushroom slices and sauté for another 3 minutes, stirring constantly until they have given off their water. Cover with cream and simmer, uncovered, until mushrooms have absorbed the cream, making a thick mixture.

With the metal blade in place, pour mushroom mixture into the beaker. Process until smooth. Season to taste with salt and pepper. Stir in Crème Fraîche or sour cream. This can be prepared ahead of time and chilled until needed. Makes about 1¾ cups.

Barley Casserole Amandine

¼ cup natural whole almonds
Water
1 large onion, quartered
¼ cup butter
½ pound mushrooms
1 cup pearl barley
Salt and pepper to taste
3 cups chicken or beef broth

Place almonds in saucepan. Cover with water and simmer for 3 minutes. Drain, cool slightly and slip off skins. Toast in 350 degree oven for about 15 minutes. With the slicing disk in place,* put the almonds in feed tube of food processor. Slice using firm pressure on the pusher. Remove and reserve for garnish.

With the metal blade in place, add the onions to the beaker. Turn machine quickly on and off 3 or 4 times, or until evenly chopped. Heat butter in a skillet. Add onions and sauté until limp, about 3 or 4 minutes. Remove from heat. Cut mushroom caps from stems. Using the metal blade, add mushroom stems to the beaker and process until chopped. Remove the metal blade, reinsert the slicing disk and stack mushroom caps in the feed tube, standing them on edge and wedging in enough so they will not tilt sideways. Slice over chopped stems using moderate pressure on the pusher. Add to onion mixture. Cook another 4 minutes, stirring occasionally. Add barley and brown it lightly, stirring to mix with other ingredients. Add salt and pepper.

Pour mixture into a buttered 1½-quart casserole. Bring broth to boil, then pour it into casserole, adding only enough to come ½ inch above barley mixture (barley floats so be careful not to add too much broth). Cover and bake in preheated 350 degree oven for 25 minutes. Add more boiling broth, if needed, and continue cooking about 20 minutes or until barley is tender and liquid is absorbed. Just before serving, sprinkle top with slivered almonds. Serve with poultry or game. Makes 6 servings.

*If you have the fine, serrated slicing disk, Part No. FP 731, use it to slice the almonds.

Salads

Coleslaw

1 small head cabbage, about 2 pounds
¾ cup mayonnaise (page 67)
½ cup sour cream
3 tablespoons wine vinegar
1 teaspoon dill seed
1 teaspoon salt
Dash freshly ground black pepper

Cut cabbage lengthwise into wedges small enough to fit in feed tube of food processor. Remove core. With the slicing disk in place, slice cabbage using moderate pressure on pusher. Transfer sliced cabbage to a large bowl and cover with ice water. Repeat until all cabbage wedges are sliced. Chill at least 2 hours. Meanwhile, with the metal blade in place, add mayonnaise, sour cream, vinegar, dill seed, salt and pepper to the beaker. Process until blended. Transfer to a jar. Cover and refrigerate. When ready to serve, drain cabbage thoroughly and toss with the dressing. Makes about 6 cups.

Egg Salad

1 celery stalk, cut in
  pieces
2 green onions, cut in
  pieces
6 hard-cooked eggs,
  halved
½ cup mayonnaise
  (page 67)
  Juice of 1 lemon
1 teaspoon salt
¼ teaspoon freshly
  ground black pepper

With metal blade in place, add celery, onions, eggs, mayonnaise, lemon juice, salt and pepper to the beaker. Process, turning on and off rapidly, until evenly chopped, about 5 to 7 seconds. If necessary, stop processing and scrape down sides with spatula. Do *not* process until smooth. Makes about 1¾ cups.

Ham Salad

1 pound cooked ham,
  cut in cubes
2 green onions, cut in
  pieces
1 celery rib, cut in
  pieces
⅔ cup mayonnaise
  (page 67)
2 tablespoons Dijon
  mustard
2 tablespoons sweet
  pickle relish
  Freshly ground black
  pepper
  Salt, if needed

With the metal blade in place, add the ham, onions and celery to beaker of food processor. Process, turning on and off rapidly, until mixture is evenly chopped, checking every few seconds. Add mayonnaise, mustard, pickle relish and pepper. Turn on and off once or twice, or until mixed. Taste and add salt, if needed. Transfer to a bowl, cover and refrigerate until ready to serve. Makes about 2½ cups.

Olive and Swiss Cheese Salad

This salad is lovely nestled on a bed of Bibb lettuce and served for lunch with cold meats. It also is especially good for picnics.

6 to 8 scallions, cut in
  pieces
2 cups stuffed green
  olives
6 ounces Gruyère or
  Swiss cheese, cut in
  pieces to fit feed tube
  Mustard Vinaigrette
  (recipe follows)

With the metal blade in place, add the scallions to the beaker. Process, turning on and off rapidly, until scallions are coarsely chopped, about 5 seconds. Carefully remove the metal blade, leaving scallions in beaker. Insert slicing disk, put olives in feed tube and slice. When disk has stopped spinning, remove it and insert shredding disk. Place cheese in feed tube and shred cheese, using moderately hard pressure on pusher. Transfer salad to a large bowl and toss with Mustard Vinaigrette. Makes 6 to 8 servings.

Mustard Vinaigrette

8 tablespoons olive or
   salad oil
1 tablespoon vinegar or
   lemon juice
1 teaspoon Dijon
   mustard
½ teaspoon black
   pepper
1 teaspoon salt

Mix all ingredients and taste. Add more vinegar or lemon juice if needed. Mix dressing with salad.

Beet Salad

This salad can be served as a first course or as an accompaniment to a main course.

2 bunches beets,
   cooked, peeled and
   quartered
6 ounces Swiss cheese,
   cut in strips to fit feed
   tube
8 celery stalks, peeled
   Vinaigrette dressings*

With the slicing disk in place, cover beaker and fill the feed tube with beet quarters, standing them upright. Slice, using firm pressure on pusher. Transfer to a bowl and marinate overnight in a mustard vinaigrette. Reinsert the slicing disk and slice cheese strips. Marinate separately in a coarse pepper vinaigrette. Slice celery in same way and marinate in a tarragon vinaigrette. The next day, just before serving, combine beets, cheese and celery and toss together well. Toss salad just before serving since beets will color other ingredients when allowed to stand. If preferred, place beets in center of salad bowl or individual serving plate and surround with mixture of cheese and celery. Makes 6 servings.

*For a basic vinaigrette dressing, use 8 tablespoons olive oil, 1 tablespoon vinegar or lemon juice, ½ teaspoon salt and ½ teaspoon pepper. Add more vinegar or lemon juice to taste. For marinating beets, add 1 teaspoon Dijon mustard; for cheese, use ¾ teaspoon coarsely ground black pepper; for celery, use tarragon vinegar.

Sauces & Salad Dressings

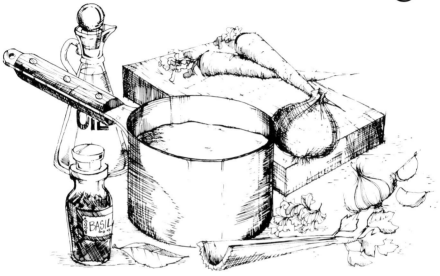

Basic Tomato Sauce

1	20-oz. can Italian plum tomatoes, drained
6	parsley sprigs
2	garlic cloves
1	carrot, cut in pieces
1	medium onion, quartered
½	celery stalk, cut in pieces
1	teaspoon sugar
1	teaspoon dried basil leaves
½	cup olive oil
1	bay leaf
1	teaspoon salt
¼	teaspoon freshly ground black pepper

With the metal blade in place, add tomatoes, parsley, garlic, carrot, onion, celery, sugar and basil to the beaker. Process, turning on and off rapidly, until ingredients are finely chopped, about 6 to 8 seconds. Pour into a large saucepan. Add olive oil, bay leaf, salt and pepper. Simmer for 45 minutes. Taste for seasoning. If a smooth sauce is desired, process mixture until puréed in the beaker, using the metal blade. Makes about 2 cups.

Marcella Hazan's Ragu alla Bolognese
(Meat Sauce as made in Bologna)

This is the classic meat sauce that has brought more glory to Bologna than almost any other accomplishment of its celebrated cuisine. It is perfection by itself with a dish of tagliatelle egg noodles, cooked al dente. It is the finest sauce you can use with lasagna and it will absolutely ennoble a dish of rigatoni, ziti or other stubby pasta. You can even serve it on toast as a hot appetizer.

1 **medium onion, quartered**
3 **tablespoons olive oil**
3 **tablespoons butter**
1 **celery stalk, cut in pieces**
1 **carrot, cut in pieces**
2 **slices prosciutto, prosciuttino or salami, cut in pieces**
1 **pound lean beef, preferably chuck, cut in cubes**
1 **teaspoon salt**
1 **cup dry white wine**
½ **cup milk**
1/8 **teaspoon nutmeg**
2 **cups canned plum tomatoes, roughly cut with their juice**

With the metal blade in place, add the onion to the beaker. Process, turning on and off, until finely chopped. Heat oil and butter in a deep earthenware or enameled cast iron casserole. Add onion and sauté until golden. With the metal blade reinserted, add celery and carrot to the beaker and process, turning on and off, until finely chopped. Add chopped mixture to sautéed onion and cook for 2 or 3 minutes, stirring frequently. With the metal blade reinserted, add ½ the ham and beef to beaker and process until chopped as fine as hamburger meat. Add chopped meat to vegetable mixture, crumbling it with a fork. Repeat with remaining ham and beef. Add salt and cook until meat has lost its raw color. Do not allow it to brown. Add wine and cook over high heat until it has evaporated. Add milk and nutmeg. Cook, stirring, until milk has evaporated. Stir in tomatoes with their juice. When sauce begins to bubble, reduce heat so that mixture cooks very slowly with just an occasional bubble breaking on the surface. Cook, covered, about 4 hours, stirring occasionally. Sauce can be kept in a tightly covered jar in the refrigerator for 5 days or frozen for longer storage. Before serving, reheat sauce at a slow simmer for 10 to 15 minutes. Makes about 2½ cups.

Hollandaise Sauce

4 **egg yolks**
2 **tablespoons lemon juice**
½ **teaspoon salt**
  Dash of Tabasco
½ **cup unsalted butter, melted**

With the metal blade in place, add egg yolks, lemon juice, salt and Tabasco to the beaker. Process for 3 seconds and, still processing, pour in bubbling melted butter. It is essential that the butter be bubbling or the sauce will not thicken. Makes about ¾ cup.

Béarnaise Sauce

This sauce should be held at room temperature for at least 30 minutes after it is made. This will give the shallots and tarragon a chance to mellow into the sauce.

2 shallots, halved
½ cup white wine
2 teaspoons dried tarragon leaves
3 egg yolks
½ teaspoon salt
½ cup sweet butter, cut in pieces

With the metal blade in place, add shallots to the beaker. Process until finely chopped. Transfer to saucepan. Add wine and tarragon. Cook over medium-high heat until reduced to almost 1 tablespoon liquid. Cool slightly. With the metal blade in place, add egg yolks and salt to the beaker. Process until thick, about 1 minute. Add cooled, reduced liquid and continue processing, adding butter 2 tablespoons at a time through the feed tube. Makes about 1 cup.

Parsley Sauce

This is a wonderful sauce to use on vegetables or on pasta.

½ cup walnuts
2 ounces Parmesan cheese, cut in ½-inch pieces
Tops of large bunch parsley (about ¾ cup tightly packed sprigs)
3 garlic cloves
⅔ cup olive oil

Blanch walnuts in boiling water for 1 minute. Dry well on paper towels. With the metal blade in place, add the cheese to the beaker. Process, turning on and off rapidly, until finely chopped. Add walnuts, parsley and garlic and process until evenly chopped. Continue processing and gradually pour olive oil through the feed tube. More olive oil may be needed if a more liquid sauce is desired. Makes about 1 cup.

Skordalia

This is a classic Greek sauce which is delicious served with fish.

2 slices white bread, torn in pieces
6 garlic cloves
2 egg yolks
¼ cup blanched whole almonds
Juice of ½ lemon (1 tablespoon)
½ cup olive oil
3 parsley sprigs

Soak bread in water; squeeze dry. With metal blade in place, add bread, garlic, egg yolks, almonds and lemon juice to beaker of food processor. Process until evenly chopped and combined, about 10 seconds. Continue processing and gradually add the oil through the feed tube to form a thick mayonnaise consistency. Add parsley and process until it is evenly chopped and distributed. Makes about ¾ cup.

Marcella Hazan's Salsa Verde per Pesce Bollito
(Green Sauce for Boiled Fish)

This sauce requires no cooking, it takes moments to prepare and it is marvelous with any kind of steamed, boiled or poached fish. It is a deep, subdued green color that looks most attractive against the opaque, white flesh of boiled fish and its gentle tartness enlivens the taste of the fish without obscuring its delicacy. If you find you like a tarter, sharper sauce, increase the quantities of lemon juice and capers.

Tops of 2 large bunches parsley (about 1½ cups tightly packed sprigs)
1 cup olive oil
¼ cup capers, drained
3 large garlic cloves
2 teaspoons lemon juice
1 teaspoon Dijon mustard
Salt

With the metal blade in place, add the parsley, olive oil, capers, garlic, lemon juice, mustard and dash of salt to the beaker. Process to a fine but not liquid consistency. Taste and add salt, if necessary. Serve at room temperature. This sauce may be prepared ahead of time and kept up to 1 week in a covered jar in the refrigerator. Always return to room temperature before serving. Makes 6 servings.

Variation: Using the metal blade, chop ¼ medium onion. Leave in beaker and add 8 flat anchovy fillets in addition to other recipe ingredients. Process as before. Serve with boiled beef, chicken, tongue and *cotechino*, a highly spiced pork sausage.

Sauce Rémoulade

6 sprigs parsley
2 tablespoons capers
2 garlic cloves
1 hard-cooked egg, quartered
1 uncooked egg
1 teaspoon salt
¼ teaspoon pepper
1½ cups olive oil

With the metal blade in place, add parsley, capers, garlic, eggs, salt and pepper to the beaker. Process until ingredients are evenly chopped, about 2 or 3 seconds. Continue processing and gradually add oil in a slow stream through feed tube. As sauce thickens, oil can be added a little faster. Makes about 1¾ cups.

Variation: For a more piquant flavor, omit salt and add 2 or 3 anchovy fillets. Taste and add salt, if needed.

Mustard Mayonnaise

Mayonnaise (page 67)
¼ cup Dijon mustard

With the metal blade in place, follow basic Mayonnaise recipe, adding Dijon mustard to the beaker. Process, adding oil as in basic recipe. Makes about 1¾ to 2 cups.

Mayonnaise

1 whole egg
1 tablespoon vinegar
  or lemon juice
1 teaspoon salt
¼ teaspoon freshly
  ground pepper
1½ cups oil

With the metal blade in place, add the egg, vinegar, salt and pepper to the beaker. Process until blended, about 2 to 3 seconds. Continue processing and gradually pour oil through feed tube, slowly at first. As mayonnaise thickens, the sound of the machine will become deeper. Taste for additional vinegar or lemon juice, salt and pepper. Transfer to a covered container and refrigerate until needed. This mayonnaise will hold for a week to 10 days in the refrigerator.

If mayonnaise should separate, pour the separated mixture into a liquid measuring cup. Using the metal blade and a clean beaker, add 2 egg yolks and process, pouring the separated mixture through the feed tube very slowly. The mayonnaise will rebind. Makes about 1¾ cups.

Anchovy Mayonnaise

8 anchovy fillets
1 egg
2 tablespoons lemon
  juice
1 tablespoon vinegar
½ teaspoon pepper
1½ cups oil

With the metal blade in place, add anchovies, egg, lemon juice, vinegar and pepper to the beaker. Process until blended, about 2 or 3 seconds. Continue processing and gradually add oil through feed tube, taking about 20 seconds to pour it in. When mayonnaise has thickened, taste for salt. Makes about 1¾ cups.

Green Mayonnaise

Mayonnaise
(page 67)
6 wilted spinach leaves
6 parsley sprigs
4 green onions, cut in
  pieces
1 teaspoon dried
  tarragon leaves *or*
3 sprigs fresh tarragon,
  stems removed
2 teaspoons dried dill weed

With the metal blade in place, follow basic Mayonnaise recipe. When mayonnaise has thickened, leave in beaker and add spinach, parsley, onions, tarragon and dill. Process, turning on and off occasionally, until ingredients are evenly chopped. Makes about 1¾ cups.

Variation: Add ¼ cup very loosely packed chives or chervil.

Mock Crème Fraîche

⅓ cup sour cream
1 cup heavy cream

With the metal blade in place, add sour cream and heavy cream to beaker of food processor. Process until well combined, about 3 seconds. Let stand in warm place until thickened, about 24 hours. Return to the beaker and process again until combined, about 2 or 3 seconds. Store in covered jar in refrigerator. Makes about 1⅓ cups.   67

Green Goddess Dressing

1¾ cups Mayonnaise
(page 67)
6 anchovy fillets
3 green onions, cut in
pieces
2 shallots, halved
2 tablespoons
tarragon vinegar
10 sprigs parsley,
stems removed
2 sprigs fresh
tarragon leaves *or*
1 teaspoon dried
tarragon leaves

With the metal blade in place, add mayonnaise, anchovy fillets, onions, shallots, vinegar, parsley and tarragon to the beaker. Process until mixture is evenly chopped, about 30 seconds. Makes about 2 cups.

Thousand Island Dressing

1 medium onion,
halved
3 tablespoons chili
sauce
2 hard-cooked eggs,
quartered
1 whole egg
1 garlic clove
1 teaspoon salt
¼ teaspoon freshly
ground black pepper
1½ cups olive oil
4 sprigs parsley
2 green onions, cut in
pieces
¼ teaspoon Tabasco

Use the shredding disk to shred onion and leave the shreds in the beaker. With the metal blade in place, add the chili sauce, 1 hard-cooked egg, the whole egg, garlic, salt and pepper to the beaker. Process, turning on and off until mixture is evenly chopped, about 5 seconds. Continue processing and slowly add oil, taking about 15 seconds to incorporate it. Mixture should thicken to mayonnaise consistency. When it does, stop processing. Add parsley, green onions, Tabasco and remaining hard-cooked egg. Turn on and off 2 or 3 times or until egg is evenly chopped. Refrigerate, covered, until needed. Makes about 2½ cups.

Bleu Cheese Vinaigrette

2 ounces bleu cheese
(about ⅓ cup firmly
packed)
½ cup olive oil
1½ tablespoons red
wine vinegar
¾ teaspoon salt
Dash freshly ground
black pepper

With the metal blade in place, process bleu cheese for 5 seconds. Add oil, vinegar, salt and pepper to the beaker. Process until well blended. Makes about ⅔ cup.

Breads

Bread Baking Basics

Before you use the food processor for bread making the first time, consider these rules.

Proofing the Yeast
If using dry yeast, measure warm (105 to 115 degrees) water or milk into a glass measuring cup. If you don't have a thermometer, mix equal amounts of boiling water and ice water. Add the yeast and sugar to the warm liquid and stir until the yeast has dissolved. With fresh yeast, temperature should be 90 to 95 degrees.

Measuring the Flour
Don't sift the flour or spoon it into a cup. Just scoop the flour directly from the package or container with a dry measuring cup and level it off with a spatula or straight-sided knife. Be sure not to heap or shake it.

Mixing in the Processor
Be careful, if too much liquid is added to the beaker of the processor, the motor slows down, overheats and shuts itself off. To prevent this, have an additional ¼ cup flour ready next to the machine. If the blade starts to lose speed, dump the ¼ cup of flour *immediately* through the feed tube. This will make the motor speed return to normal. Be cautious with liquids — you may not need the entire amount and at times you may need more. If you do — dribble it in slowly, stopping as soon as a ball of dough forms on top of the processor blade.

Kneading
On a lightly floured board, flatten the dough slightly with floured hands or hand. Push the dough away from you with the heels of your hands. Fold and rotate the dough a quarter turn. Repeat folding, pushing, turning, until the dough is elastic and is not sticky. You may — if the dough seems too loose — have to knead in additional flour.

First Rising
Place the kneaded dough in a large greased bowl. Turn the dough to grease all sides. Cover the bowl with plastic wrap and allow the dough to rise in a warm (80 to 85 degree) draft-free place, for instance an electric oven with a quart of boiling water on the

bottom shelf or a gas oven with the pilot light on.

To find out whether the dough has risen enough, insert a finger about ½ inch into the dough. If the indentation remains, the dough has risen enough.

Punching Down
Now whack your fist into the center of the dough. Turn out on a lightly floured board. Knead a few times. You are now ready to shape except for our recipes made with rye and whole wheat flours. These need a second rising in the bowl before shaping.

Shaping a Loaf
Roll or pat the dough into a rectangle with the short side as long as the bread pan you are using. Starting from a short side, roll the dough tightly jelly-roll style. With the side of the hand, pinch each end to seal, then fold the ends under.

Rising After Shaping
Place loaf seam side down in a greased pan, cover as before, and allow to rise in a warm place until double in bulk. To test, press a finger lightly into the loaf near the edge. If the dent remains, the loaf is ready to bake.

Selecting Pan Size
Generally, if a pan is filled ⅔ full, you will have a nicely shaped loaf after baking. Our recipes indicate the cup capacity of the bread pan. If you wish to find the capacity of your pan, fill it with water from a liquid measuring cup, noting how much water you had to add to fill the pan.

Testing for Doneness
When the baking time is up, remove the bread from the pan and tap the bottom or sides with your knuckles or a wooden spoon. It sounds hollow, if it's done. Place the bread on a wire rack to cool completely before storing. Sometimes, if you want a better-done crust, slip the loaf out of the pan back to the oven for a few minutes.

Storing
Store completely cooled bread in a plastic bag and seal with a wire twist. Store at room temperature. If you freeze the bread, allow it to come to room temperature before unwrapping.

Brioche Loaf

1 **package active dry yeast**
¼ **cup warm milk**
1 **tablespoon sugar**
2 **cups unbleached all-purpose flour**
1 **teaspoon salt**
½ **cup *frozen* butter, cut in 8 pieces**
2 **eggs, lightly beaten**

Proof yeast in warm milk with sugar. With the metal blade in place, add flour, salt and butter to the beaker. Process until butter is cut into flour mixture, about 20 seconds. Add yeast mixture and process until combined, about 5 seconds. Add eggs and process until ball of dough forms on blades. Turn out onto lightly floured board and knead until smooth, about 1 to 2 minutes. Place in greased bowl, turning to coat all sides. Cover and let rise in warm place until doubled in bulk, about 1½ to 2 hours. Punch down, knead several times, shape into a loaf and place in a well-buttered 5-cup loaf pan. Cover and let rise until doubled, about 1 hour. If desired, brush with a glaze made by beating 1 egg yolk with 1 tablespoon cream or milk. Bake in preheated 350 degree oven for 35 to 40 minutes. Makes 1 loaf.

Corn Bread

1 cup flour
1 cup cornmeal
1 tablespoon baking powder
1 teaspoon salt
¼ cup butter, cut in pieces
1 cup milk
2 eggs

With the metal blade in place, add flour, cornmeal, baking powder, salt and butter to the beaker. Process until butter is completely cut into flour mixture, about 20 seconds. While processing, pour milk through feed tube all at once. Add eggs, one at a time, processing until mixture is well blended. Pour batter into a buttered 8x8x2-inch pan and bake in preheated 400 degree oven for 25 to 30 minutes. Cut into squares. Makes 9 servings.

Mustard Mixed Grain Bread

This is a great sandwich bread, especially good for cold meats. It is a wonderfully perfumed loaf with the aroma of mustard emanating not only from the oven during baking, but also from the bread itself in a sandwich.

2 packages active dry yeast
½ cup warm water
1½ teaspoons sugar
1⅓ cups unbleached all-purpose flour
⅔ cup rye flour
⅔ cup whole wheat flour
1 teaspoon salt
3 tablespoons butter, cut in 3 or more pieces
½ cup Dijon mustard
¼ cup warm water

Proof yeast in ½ cup warm water with sugar. With the metal blade in place, add flours, salt and butter to the beaker. Process until butter is cut into flour mixture, about 20 seconds. Add mustard and process until evenly distributed. Scrape down sides of beaker. Add yeast mixture and process until combined. Continue processing, dribbling in remaining ¼ cup water only until ball of dough forms on blades (all the water may not be necessary). This will be a heavy, very sticky dough because of the rye flour. Place in greased bowl, turning to coat all sides. Cover and let rise in warm place until doubled in bulk, about 1½ hours. Punch down, knead several times, return to bowl and let rise a second time until doubled, about 1 hour. Punch down and knead for 1 to 2 minutes. Allow to rest 10 minutes. Shape into a loaf and place in a buttered 5-cup loaf pan. Cover and let rise until doubled. Slash top in 2 or 3 places. If desired, brush with a glaze made by beating 1 egg white with 1 tablespoon water. Bake in preheated 375 degree oven for 35 to 40 minutes. Makes 1 loaf.

Rye Bread

This is an excellent rye bread and it is especially good for sandwiches. It will keep for 4 or 5 days, if tightly wrapped and stored in the refrigerator.

1 **package active dry yeast**
¼ **cup warm milk**
2 **teaspoons sugar**
1½ **cups unbleached all-purpose flour**
1½ **cups rye flour**
1 **teaspoon salt**
2 **tablespoons butter**
¾ **cup warm water**

Proof yeast in warm milk with sugar. With the metal blade in place, add flours, salt and butter to the beaker. Process until butter is cut into flour mixture, about 20 seconds. Add yeast mixture and process until combined, about 5 seconds. Continue processing and pour a scant ½ cup warm water through feed tube, then dribble in only enough of the remaining water for a ball of dough to form on blades (the whole ¼ cup of water may not be necessary). Turn out onto lightly floured board and knead until smooth and satiny, about 2 minutes. Place in greased bowl, turning to coat all sides. Cover and let rise in warm place until doubled in bulk, about 1½ hours. Punch down, knead several times, return to bowl and let rise a second time until doubled, about 1 hour. Punch down and knead several times. Shape into a loaf and place in a buttered 5-cup loaf pan. Cover and let rise a third time. Bake in preheated 375 degree oven for 35 to 40 minutes. Makes 1 loaf.

Orange Bread

This bread makes an extraordinary toast for breakfast, especially if you are a cinnamon toast lover. It has an incredible texture and much of the orange flavor disappears during baking, leaving just slight acidity. Many people interpret the orange flavor as an egg content which it obviously does not have.

1 **package active dry yeast**
¼ **cup warm water**
1 **tablespoon sugar**
2½ **cups unbleached all-purpose flour**
2 **tablespoons sugar**
1 **teaspoon salt**
3 **tablespoons butter, cut in 3 or more pieces**
⅔ **cup orange juice, at room temperature**

Proof yeast in warm water with 1 tablespoon sugar. With the metal blade in place, add flour, 2 tablespoons sugar, salt and butter to the beaker. Process until butter is cut into flour mixture, about 20 seconds. Add yeast mixture and process until combined, about 5 seconds. Continue processing and pour ⅓ cup orange juice through feed tube, then dribble in additional orange juice only until ball of dough forms on blades (all the orange juice may not be necessary). Turn out onto lightly floured board and knead until smooth and satiny, about 2 to 3 minutes. Place in greased bowl, turning to coat all sides. Cover and let rise in warm place until doubled in bulk, about 1 to 2 hours. Punch down, knead several times, shape into a loaf and place in a buttered 5-cup loaf pan. Cover and let rise until doubled, about 1 hour. Bake in preheated 375 degree oven for 30 minutes. Makes 1 loaf.

Pastries & Crêpes

Sour Cream Pastry

2¼ **cups all-purpose flour**
¾ **cup *frozen* butter, cut in 1-tablespoon pieces**
3 **tablespoons sour cream**
1 **egg**
½ **teaspoon salt**

With metal blade in place, add flour, butter, sour cream, egg and salt to the beaker. Process, turning on and off, for 15 seconds. Continue processing until ball of dough forms on blades. This dough should be somewhat soft. Wrap quickly in waxed paper or foil and chill in refrigerator until firm enough to roll out. If too firm to roll out, let warm slightly at room temperature. Makes two 8 or 9-inch pastry shells.

Puff Pastry

3 cups all-purpose
   flour
¼ cup *frozen* butter,
   cut in 1-tablespoon
   pieces
1 teaspoon salt
1 cup ice water
1½ cups cold butter, cut
   in 1-tablespoon
   pieces
½ cup all-purpose flour

With metal blade in place, add the 3 cups flour, frozen butter and salt to the beaker of the food processor. Process, turning on and off, until butter is cut into flour. Continue processing, adding ice water through feed tube, until ball of dough forms on blades. Remove and refrigerate for 30 minutes.

Prepare butter mixture for rolling between layers of pastry. With metal blade in place, add the cold butter and the ½ cup flour to the beaker. Process, turning on and off and scraping down sides occasionally, until butter begins to form a dough. Do not overprocess or butter will become too soft. If necessary, scrape mixture from sides of beaker once or twice during processing. This should take 10 to 15 seconds. Refrigerate for 30 minutes. Proceed as you would to make puff pastry from your favorite recipe.

Pâte Brisée

2 cups all-purpose flour
½ cup *frozen* butter, cut
   in 1-tablespoon
   pieces
¼ teaspoon salt
2 whole eggs
1 tablespoon lemon
   juice

With metal blade in place, add flour, butter and salt to beaker of food processor. Process, turning on and off rapidly, until butter is cut into flour and very small granules are formed, about 10 seconds. Add eggs and lemon juice. Continue processing until ball of dough forms on blades. If dough seems too soft, sprinkle with 1 to 2 tablespoons flour and process until combined, about 6 seconds. Refrigerate and use as you would any recipe calling for Pâte Brisée. Makes two 8 or 9-inch pastry shells.

Pâte Sucrée

Use in any recipe that calls for a sweet pastry shell.

1 cup all-purpose flour
6 tablespoons *frozen*
   butter, cut in
   1-tablespoon pieces
2 tablespoons sugar
1 egg yolk
1 tablespoon cold
   water
1/8 teaspoon salt

With metal blade in place, add flour, butter, sugar, egg yolk, water and salt to the beaker. Process, turning on and off rapidly, for 5 seconds. Continue processing until ball of dough forms on blades. Makes one 8 or 9-inch pastry shell.

Very Short Pastry

This makes a very flaky, rich pastry for pies and top crusts.

2 cups all-purpose flour
1 cup *frozen* butter, cut in 1-tablespoon pieces
1 egg
1 tablespoon heavy cream
1 teaspoon salt

With the metal blade in place, add flour, butter, egg, cream and salt to beaker of food processor. Process, turning on and off rapidly, for 15 seconds. Continue processing until ball of dough forms on blades. Chill ½ hour. For a very flaky pastry, roll pastry into a rectangle approximately 16 x 8 inches, then fold in thirds as you would a letter. This is the same folding used in classic puff pastry. Repeat, rolling out and folding into thirds 2 more times. Chill at least 1 hour before using. Makes two 8 or 9-inch pastry shells.

Rich Tart Pastry

This rich tart pastry is especially good for fruit tarts: apple, raspberry, strawberry, pineapple.

2 cups all-purpose flour
¾ cup *frozen* butter, cut in 1-tablespoon pieces
3 tablespoons sugar
3 hard-cooked egg yolks
1 egg
1½ tablespoons grated lemon peel
1 tablespoon cold water
½ teaspoon salt

With metal blade in place, add flour, butter, sugar, egg yolks, egg, lemon peel, water and salt to beaker of food processor. Process, turning on and off rapidly, for 15 seconds. Continue processing until ball of dough forms on blades. Makes two 8 or 9-inch tart pastry shells.

Lard Crust

This crust can be used anytime you need a lard crust, whether it be for a sweet dessert or for a meat pie of any kind.

2 cups all-purpose flour
6 tablespoons *frozen* lard, cut in 1-tablespoon pieces
7 tablespoons cold water
¼ teaspoon salt

With the metal blade in place, add flour, lard, water and salt to beaker of food processor. Process, turning on and off, for 5 seconds. Continue processing until ball of dough forms on blades. If dough feels slightly soft, sprinkle with 2 tablespoons flour and process again. Chill for 1 hour before using. Makes two 8 or 9-inch pastry shells.

Whole Wheat Pastry

This is a marvelous recipe which is especially good for a savory quiche. It goes wonderfully with certain chicken and meat pies.

2 **cups whole wheat flour**
8 **tablespoons** *frozen* **lard, cut in 1-tablespoon pieces**
8 **tablespoons cold water**
¼ **teaspoon salt**

With the metal blade in place, add flour, lard, water and salt to beaker of food processor. Process, turning on and off, for 5 seconds. Continue processing until ball of dough forms on blades. Makes two 8 or 9-inch pastry shells.

Basic Crêpes

This crêpes recipe can be used anytime you need crêpes. It can be sweet or savory.

1 **cup minus 2 tablespoons all-purpose flour**
3 **eggs**
2 **tablespoons melted butter**
½ **teaspoon salt**
1½ **cups milk (about)**

With the metal blade in place, add the flour, eggs, butter and salt to the beaker. Process, gradually pouring milk through feed tube, until batter has consistency of light cream. Let batter rest for 2 hours before using.

To make crêpes, butter a 6-inch pan with rounded sides. Place pan over medium-high heat until butter sizzles. Pour a little batter into pan, tilting and rotating so batter coats surface evenly. Pour any excess batter back into bowl. Cook crêpes until lightly browned on underside, then turn and brown other side. Remove from pan and keep warm in low oven, covered with foil, until ready to use.

For sweet crêpes, add 1 tablespoon sugar and the scrapings of a 1-inch piece of vanilla bean to beaker with the flour. Makes about 14 crêpes.

Desserts

Apricot Sherbet

½ pound dried apricots
2 cups sugar
2 cups warm water

Soak apricots in water for 2 hours. Drain thoroughly. In a large saucepan, combine apricots, sugar and water. Bring to boil, then reduce heat and simmer until apricots are tender, about 30 minutes. With the metal blade in place, add apricots and about 1 cup of the apricot syrup to beaker of food processor. Process, turning on and off occasionally, until a smooth purée is formed, about 30 seconds. Continue processing and gradually pour remaining apricot syrup through feed tube. Remove beaker from base immediately and pour into canister of an ice cream freezer. (If desired, first press apricot purée through a fine sieve.) Freeze according to manufacturer's directions. Makes about 1 quart.

Barbara Kafka's Strawberry Bavarian Cream

Barbara Kafka's greatest pleasure in food seems to come from the rich and varied tastes of fresh produce, fully and naturally ripe. Her special pleasure in the food processor comes from the use it enables her to make of seasonal fruits and vegetables with their raw splendor shining through.

The secret of this recipe is that the strawberries are uncooked and, hence, do not discolor or change flavor. Use the ripest strawberries you can find. Size doesn't matter.

3 pints strawberries, washed, dried and hulled

¼ to 1 cup granulated sugar

Juice of 1 lemon, strained (optional)

Jigger of Triple Sec (optional)

3 envelopes unflavored gelatin

½ cup cold water

3 cups day-old heavy, sweet cream, chilled

With the metal blade in place, add 1 pint strawberries to the beaker of food processor. Process for 1 minute. Add second pint of strawberries and process for another minute. Add remaining strawberries and process until a liquid purée has formed. If desired, press through a fine sieve to remove seeds. Transfer strawberries to a stainless steel bowl. Gradually add sugar to strawberry purée, mixing well and tasting. If additional flavor is desired, add lemon juice and Triple Sec.

Sprinkle gelatin on cold water in measuring cup. Place cup in saucepan with water coming ½ way up cup. Place over medium heat until gelatin dissolves, scraping sides of cup occasionally with spatula. Add dissolved gelatin to strawberry purée* and mix thoroughly. If every granule of gelatin does not dissolve, pour it through a fine sieve into strawberry mixture.

Place bowl with strawberry-gelatin mixture in a large bowl filled with ice. Stir from sides of bowl from time to time until mixture begins to thicken. With the metal blade in place, add 1 cup cream to the beaker. Process until whipped, about 30 seconds. Transfer to a bowl and repeat with remaining cream, whipping 1 cup at a time. Fold cream into strawberry mixture until thoroughly mixed. Rinse a 2½-quart mold with ice water and dry. Fill mold with strawberry-cream mixture. Cover with plastic wrap and chill for about 1 hour. If made a day ahead, let stand at room temperature about 15 minutes before serving. Briefly dip mold in a large bowl containing very hot water. Invert a serving plate over mold, then turn both together and lift off mold. Serve with a light Moselle wine and additional whipped cream and strawberries, if desired. Makes 8 servings.

*Make sure strawberry purée is at room temperature. If too cold, the gelatin will set too fast and become stringy.

Almond Cream Puffs

½ **cup natural whole almonds**
Water
½ **cup hot water**
¼ **cup butter**
¼ **teaspoon sugar**
¼ **teaspoon salt**
½ **cup flour**
2 **eggs**
1 **egg, beaten**
Coffee Pastry Cream (recipe follows)

Place the almonds in a saucepan. Cover with water and simmer for 3 minutes. Drain, cool slightly and slip off skins. With the metal blade in place, add the almonds to beaker. Process until coarsely chopped.

Combine the hot water, butter, sugar and salt in a saucepan. Bring to boil, stirring occasionally. Reduce heat and add flour all at once, stirring vigorously until flour is absorbed and mixture leaves sides of pan and forms a ball. Remove from heat and let cool for about 5 minutes.

Reinsert the metal blade. Transfer batter to the beaker and add the 2 eggs. Process until smooth and shiny, about 30 to 45 seconds. The mixture will be very thick. Add almonds and turn on and off quickly 2 or 3 times to distribute nuts evenly.

Drop rounded tablespoons of mixture on an ungreased baking sheet, leaving 2 inches between puffs to allow room for expansion during baking. Brush tops with the beaten egg and set aside for 5 minutes before baking.

Bake in preheated 425 degree oven for 10 minutes. Reduce heat to 375 degrees and bake about 30 minutes longer. Remove from oven and make a 1-inch slit in the side of each puff. Cool on wire racks. When ready to serve, cut off tops, fill with Coffee Pastry Cream and replace tops. Makes 8 to 10 puffs.

Variation: Sprinkle tops of puffs with additional chopped nuts before brushing with egg glaze.

Coffee Pastry Cream

2 **cups milk**
1½ **teaspoons instant coffee**
½ **cup sugar**
4 **egg yolks**
½ **cup minus 1 tablespoon flour**
½ **teaspoon cornstarch**
½ **teaspoon vanilla**

Heat milk with instant coffee in saucepan, stirring to dissolve coffee. Beat sugar and egg yolks together in another saucepan. Add flour and cornstarch and mix thoroughly. Place over low heat and gradually add hot milk mixture, stirring continuously. Cook, stirring, until smooth and thick. Remove from heat and cool before adding vanilla. Cover surface with plastic wrap or buttered waxed paper to prevent a skin from forming. Makes about 2½ cups.

Brazilian Avocado Cream Dessert

2 **large avocados**
¾ **cup sugar**
¼ **cup heavy cream**
¼ **cup lime juice**
¼ **teaspoon salt**

With the metal blade in place, add the avocados, sugar, cream, lime juice and salt to the beaker. Process, turning on and off, until evenly chopped, about 15 seconds. Scrape down sides with a spatula. Continue processing until smooth. Pour into individual molds and chill for at least 4 hours. Makes 4 servings.

Chocolate Mousse

This can be served as a frozen mousse by pouring it into a decorative mold and freezing it for 6 hours. Or, it may be poured into individual cups and served as you would a Pot de Crème au Chocolate.

¼ **cup sugar**
⅓ **cup water**
1½ **cups heavy cream**
1 **6-oz. package semisweet chocolate pieces**
3 **tablespoons dark rum**
3 **egg yolks**
½ **cup toasted almonds**

Combine sugar and water in small saucepan and boil for 3 minutes. With the metal blade in place, add cream to the beaker of the food processor. Process uninterrupted until a very thick whipped cream forms, about 1 minute. Transfer to a large bowl. Without washing beaker, reinsert metal blade and add chocolate pieces. Process, turning on and off, for 15 to 20 seconds. Continue processing and gradually pour in hot syrup, rum and egg yolks. Add almonds. Process, turning on and off, until almonds are coarsely chopped and evenly distributed, about 20 seconds. Using a spatula, scrape chocolate-almond mixture over whipped cream and fold together. Freeze or chill before serving. Makes 6 servings.

Apricot Pudding

Apricot pudding makes a beautiful presentation when topped with whipped cream, which has been lightly flavored with Grand Marnier or Cointreau, or a little orange water, and then lightly sprinkled with chopped pistachio nuts.

½ **pound dried apricots**
1¼ **cups white wine**
2 **pieces (each 1-inch square) lemon peel**
1½ **tablespoons arrowroot**
½ **cup butter, cut in pieces**
⅔ **cup sugar**
6 **egg yolks**
6 **egg whites**

Stew apricots in white wine until tender. With the metal blade in place, add apricot mixture and lemon peel to beaker of food processor. Process, turning on and off rapidly, until evenly chopped, about 8 seconds. Add arrowroot, butter, sugar and egg yolks. Process until completely smooth, turning on and off, if necessary. Beat egg whites until stiff, but not dry, then fold into apricot purée. Pour into buttered 6-cup soufflé dish and cover with a piece of buttered aluminum foil. Place in water bath and bake in preheated 350 degree oven for 50 minutes. Cool slightly before serving. Makes 8 servings.

Helen McCully's Praliné Powder

This delicious powder is used in desserts (soufflés, for example), sauces, over ice cream and as a flavoring in frostings and cake fillings.

1½ cups granulated sugar
½ cup water
1 cup blanched almonds, skins removed
1 cup filberts, skins removed

Combine sugar and water in heavy saucepan. Place over medium heat. Add nuts. Cook, stirring with wooden spoon, until sugar dissolves and mixture becomes a light golden caramel color. Immediately remove from heat and pour onto a lightly-oiled baking sheet. When cold, break into 1-inch pieces. With the metal blade in place, add praliné pieces to the beaker. Process, turning on and off, until evenly pulverized to desired fineness (coarsely for ice creams and fine for soufflés and sauces). Store in an airtight container in the refrigerator. Makes about 3½ cups.

Praliné Butter Cream

To make Praliné Butter Cream, stir 4 tablespoons praliné powder into 1 cup butter cream. Use as a filling between layers of cake.

Del Mar Mist

The Del Mar Ranch in the Monterey Valley of California is part of a newly organized wine producing company, the Monterey Vineyards. This ice is something we made one afternoon in class with Gerald Asher, who represents the Monterey Vineyards. It is excellent either as a dessert or between the fish and meat courses as you would serve a champagne sorbet.

1 bottle Del Mar Ranch or other fruity white wine
2 cups sugar
Juice and zest of 1 lemon

In saucepan, combine the wine, sugar and juice and zest of lemon. Bring to a boil. Reduce heat and simmer for 1 minute. Cool to room temperature, then pour into 2 ice cube trays and freeze. Just before serving, with the metal blade in place, add frozen cubes to beaker of food processor, 1 tray at a time. Process, turning on and off rapidly, for 2 or 3 minutes until an absolutely fine mist-like ice, free of all lumps, forms. Spoon into individual cups and serve immediately. Makes 6 to 8 servings.

Steamed Fig Pudding

6 to 7 slices white bread, quartered *or* enough to make 3 cups crumbs
½ cup milk
1 cup beef suet, cut in pieces
½ pound (about 1½ cups) dried figs, stemmed and quartered
3 eggs
1 cup sugar
Hard Sauce (recipe follows)

With the metal blade in place, add the bread to the beaker. Process until coarse crumbs are formed. Spread out on jelly-roll pan and let dry in slow oven (300 degrees) for about 4 to 5 minutes. Transfer to large bowl. Add milk and mix to soften. Reinsert metal blade and add the suet, figs and eggs to the beaker of processor. Process, turning on and off rapidly, until mixture is evenly chopped. Add bread crumbs and sugar. Continue processing until mixture resembles a paste. Pour into a 6-cup pudding mold* or container and cover tightly. If there is not a cover, use 2 sheets of aluminum foil and fasten with string. Place on rack in kettle and fill with boiling water to a depth ⅔ up the mold. Cover kettle and steam pudding 3 hours or more, replenishing boiling water as needed. Unmold pudding and serve with Hard Sauce. Makes 6 servings.

*When using a mold or container without a handle, be certain there will be a way to remove the mold from the boiling water when the pudding is cooked.

Hard Sauce

¾ cup butter, cut in 1-tablespoon pieces
½ cups confectioners sugar
Dash of salt
1 tablespoon brandy or rum

With the metal blade in place, add butter, sugar and salt to the beaker. Process until combined. Still processing, add brandy through feed tube and continue until mixture is smooth. Makes about 1 cup.

Pound Cake

1 cup butter, cut in pieces
¾ cup sugar
4 egg yolks
2 tablespoons Scotch
1 teaspoon vanilla
½ teaspoon salt
¼ teaspoon baking powder
2 cups all-purpose flour
4 egg whites
¼ cup sugar

With the metal blade in place, add butter and the ¾ cup sugar to the beaker. Process, turning on and off, until mixture is creamed, about 15 to 20 seconds. Add egg yolks, one at a time, and process after each until well combined. Add the Scotch, vanilla, salt and baking powder. Process until combined, about 5 seconds. Add flour and flick machine on and off 4 or 5 times until flour just disappears. In a bowl, beat egg whites until soft peaks form. Continue to beat, gradually adding the ¼ cup sugar, until stiff, but not dry. Pour batter from beaker over whites and fold carefully into whites. Pour into a well-greased 6-cup Bundt or loaf pan. Bake in preheated 300 degree oven for 1¼ to 1½ hours or until toothpick inserted in center comes out clean. Makes 1 cake, about 2 pounds.   83

Maurice Moore-Betty's Strawberry Tart

Pâte Sucrée (page 75)
1 8-oz. can almond paste
1 egg yolk
2 tablespoons sweet butter
¼ cup red currant jelly
2 tablespoons water
Pinch of sugar
1 to 1½ pints fresh strawberries, washed, dried and hulled
Confectioners sugar

Prepare Pâte Sucrée. Place an 8-inch flan ring* on a baking sheet. Roll out pastry to a circle about 1/8-inch thick. Roll pastry onto rolling pin, then unroll it over the flan ring. Press pastry neatly into bottom edge of ring and prick all over with a fork. Bake in a preheated 425 degree oven for 10 to 12 minutes. Remove from oven and while hot, trim edge with a sharp, heavy knife.

With the metal blade in place, add the almond paste, egg yolk and butter to the beaker. Process until smooth. Scrape into cooled pastry shell and spread evenly over bottom. In small saucepan, stir jelly with water and sugar over low heat until melted. Arrange berries on almond paste, covering it completely. If berries are large, cut them in quarters from tip to stem and arrange them close together so they appear whole. Brush with jelly glaze. If made ahead, remove from refrigerator at least 30 minutes before serving time. Sprinkle lightly with confectioners sugar just before serving. Makes 6 to 8 servings.

*An 8-inch pie plate or quiche pan may be substituted for the flan ring.

Nut Butter Balls

1 cup almonds, filberts, pecans or walnuts
1 cup sifted all-purpose flour
2 to 3 tablespoons sugar
½ cup butter, cut in 1-tablespoon pieces
½ teaspoon vanilla or
2 teaspoons bourbon, brandy or rum
Confectioners sugar

Toast nuts in preheated 325 degree oven for 5 to 8 minutes to bring out full flavor. With the metal blade in place, add flour, nuts, sugar, butter and vanilla to the beaker. Process until blended, about 30 seconds. Scrape down with spatula and process again until ball of dough forms on blades, about 15 seconds. Turn out onto lightly floured board. Take small portions of dough and roll into ropes about 1 inch in diameter. Cut into even bite-size pieces, roll between palms of hands into balls and place on ungreased baking sheets. Bake in preheated 325 degree oven for 12 to 15 minutes. Let cool 3 to 5 minutes on baking sheets, then transfer to wire racks to cool completely. While warm, sift confectioners sugar over them or shake, a few at a time, in a bag containing confectioners sugar. This will give them a heavy coating of sugar. If less sugar is desired, wait until they cool before adding sugar. Makes about 4 dozen.

Raspberry or Strawberry Fool

1 quart raspberries or
  strawberries
1 cup sugar (about)
1 cup heavy cream,
  whipped until soft
  peaks are formed *or*
1½ cups commercial
  sour cream

With the metal blade in place, add ⅓ the raspberries or strawberries to the beaker. Process, turning on and off rapidly, until puréed, about 8 to 10 seconds. If using raspberries, force puréed raspberries through a fine sieve to remove seeds. Repeat until all the berries are puréed. Sweeten to taste. Fold puréed berries into whipped cream or sour cream. Chill until very cold. Serve in small glasses along with thin butter cookies or fingers of shortbread. Makes 6 to 8 servings.

Variations: Frozen berries, with some of the syrup poured off, may be substituted for the fresh berries. You may want to flavor them with a little lemon juice. Yogurt may be used in place of the whipped cream or sour cream. If desired, add ½ teaspoon vanilla extract to the whipped cream.

Orange Ice

1 2-inch square orange
  peel
4 cups freshly
  squeezed orange
  juice
1 cup sugar
⅓ cup Grand Marnier

With the metal blade in place, add orange peel, 1 cup orange juice, sugar and Grand Marnier to beaker of food processor. Process until combined, about 15 seconds. Add processed ingredients to remaining 3 cups orange juice and mix well. Pour into 2 ice cube trays and freeze. Just before serving, with the metal blade in place, add frozen cubes, 1 tray at a time, to beaker of food processor. Process, turning on and off rapidly, until a fine ice, free of all lumps, forms, about 2 to 3 minutes. Serve immediately. Makes 4 to 6 servings.

Peanut Raisin Balls

¾ cup Crunchy Peanut
  Spread (page 21)
3 tablespoons honey
½ cup non-fat dry milk
  powder
½ cup raisins
  Madeira wine
  (optional)

With the metal blade in place, add the peanut spread and honey to beaker of food processor. Process until thoroughly mixed, about 3 to 5 seconds. Add milk powder and process until mixture forms a ball on blades, about 6 seconds. Transfer to a bowl and knead in raisins, which for additional flavor may be soaked overnight in Madeira wine, then dried thoroughly before being kneaded in. Roll into balls the size of hazelnuts and refrigerate at least 30 minutes before serving. Makes 25 to 30.

Accompaniments

Apple Chutney

This chutney, which goes beautifully with lamb and is especially good with Indian curry dishes, will keep for several months if tightly covered and refrigerated

12 tart apples (4 pounds) peeled, cored and quartered
2 large green peppers, seeded and quartered
2 large onions, quartered
1 3-oz. can peeled green chili peppers, seeded
3 garlic cloves
½ cup fresh ginger, cut in pieces
2 teaspoons salt
½ teaspoon cayenne
3½ cups brown sugar
2½ cups cider vinegar
1½ cups raisins

Place apples in large bowl with very slightly salted water to prevent discoloring. With the slicing disk in place, fill feed tube with apple quarters, standing them upright. Process, using moderate pressure on pusher. Transfer apple slices to large kettle. With the metal chopping blade in place, add green peppers, onions, green chilies, garlic, ginger, salt and cayenne to beaker. Process, turning on and off rapidly, until finely chopped, about 10 to 15 seconds. Add chopped ingredients, brown sugar, vinegar and raisins to apples. Cook, uncovered, over low heat, stirring frequently, for about 3 hours to make a thick, rich chutney. Makes about 8 cups.

Pear Sauce

This is a pleasant switch from applesauce and it may be used in any way that applesauce is used. It may be sprinkled with nutmeg or cinnamon and served as a dessert or accompaniment to meats.

6 slightly underripe
  pears, peeled, cored
  and quartered
1 lemon, peeled, seeded
  and quartered
1 to 2 cups sugar

With the metal blade in place, add ½ the pears and ½ the lemon to beaker of food processor. Process, turning on and off rapidly, until evenly chopped, about 30 seconds. Transfer to a large saucepan. Repeat with remaining pears and lemon. Add 1 cup sugar to pear mixture. Cook slowly for 30 minutes. Taste and, if necessary, add more sugar. Cook slowly until sauce has consistency of thick applesauce, about 1 to 1½ hours. Makes about 1½ cups.

Helen McCully's Version of James Beard's Cranberry Relish

Cranberries never looked so pretty and never tasted better.

1 pound (4 cups) fresh
  cranberries
1 small navel orange,
  quartered with peel
  left on
1 to 1½ cups sugar
3 tablespoons bourbon
  or Grand Marnier

With the metal blade in place, add ½ the cranberries and ½ the orange pieces to beaker of food processor. Process, turning on and off rapidly, until mixture is evenly chopped to desired texture. Transfer to a bowl. Repeat with remaining cranberries and orange pieces. Return first batch to beaker. Add 1 cup sugar and bourbon or Grand Marnier. Process to mix. Taste and add more sugar, if desired. Store in an airtight container in the refrigerator. Makes about 3½ cups.

Loni Kuhn's Red Pepper Jelly

This red pepper jelly has many uses and it is a great garnish for roast pork or beef.

½ pounds red bell
  peppers, quartered
  and seeded
2 teaspoons chili
  powder
2 cups cider vinegar
⅔ cup lemon juice
2 teaspoons salt
10 cups sugar
1 6-oz. bottle fruit
  pectin

With the metal blade in place, add ⅓ the red peppers and chili powder to the beaker. Process, turning on and off rapidly, until evenly chopped. Scrape down. Continue processing until mixture becomes liquid with tiny bits of pepper. Transfer to a large kettle. Repeat twice with remaining peppers and chili powder. Add cider vinegar, lemon juice and salt to pepper mixture. Boil rapidly for 10 minutes. Stir in sugar. Return to boil and boil for 5 minutes, skimming occasionally. Stir in fruit pectin and boil for 1 minute. Reduce heat, skim again as needed, and ladle into hot sterilized jars. Seal with melted paraffin. Makes about 6 pints.

Index

Index

Index

Notes